In Our Hands

A Peace and Social Justice Program
Adults

Robert C. Branch

Samuel Goldenberg

Mary Thomson

with

Barry Andrews, Pat Hoertdoerfer, Eleanor Hunting,

Virginia Lane, Harold Rosen

David Marshak, Developmental Editor

Judith Frediani, Project Editor

A Project of the Peace and Social Justice Curriculum Team

Unitarian Universalist Association

© 1990 by the Unitarian Universalist Association,
25 Beacon St., Boston, MA 02108.
All rights reserved.
Printed in U.S.A.
ISBN 1-55896-161-5

Permission is granted to photocopy all the Handouts and the Optional Passages.

Production Editor: Kathy Wolff
Text Designer: Suzanne Morgan
Cover Designer: Lisa Clark
Editorial Assistant: Timothy Reynolds
Cover Art: Dr. Charlie Clements Peace Quilt © Boise Peace Quilt Project. Used by permission.

Acknowledgments

We want to recognize the contribution made to the work of the Peace and Social Justice Curriculum Team by Mary Madison during her tenure on the team in 1984-85.

We wish to acknowledge the significant contribution made to the development of this program by all of the Unitarian Universalists, leaders and participants, who took part in the curriculum's field test. These field testers were members of the following congregations: the First Universalist Society of Bangor, Maine; the Arlington Street Church of Boston, Massachusetts; the West Shore Unitarian Universalist Church of Cleveland, Ohio; the First Unitarian Church of Richmond, Virginia; and the Michael Servetus Unitarian Fellowship of Vancouver, Washington.

The words of Charlotte Perkins Gilman, used in Optional Passages, are reprinted from *The Living of Charlotte Perkins Gilman: An Autobiography* by permission of Ayer Co. Publishers, 382 Main St., P. O. Box 958, Salem, NH 03079. The quotation from Peter Raible, also in Optional Passages, is used with the author's permission. We are grateful to *The American Theosophist* for use of the Richard Falk quotation.

Finally, we want to thank the members of the UUA Religious Education Advisory Committee and the members of the Department of Religious Education for their contributions to the development of this program.

Contents

Introduction to *In Our Hands* 1

Introduction to *Adults* 5

Session 1: Orientation and Beginnings 9

Session 2: What Is the State of Peace and Justice in the World? 13

Session 3: Do We Choose Peace and Justice? 17

Session 4: How Do We Live a Just and Peaceful Life with Others? 21

Session 5: What Are Our Visions of a Just and Peaceful World? 25

Session 6: How Do We Make a More Just and Peaceful World? 29

Optional Passages 33

Handout 1: "Program Outline" 37

Handout 2: "Program Goals" 38

Handout 3: "Unitarian Universalist Principles" 39

Handout 4: "Guidelines for Your Peace and Justice Story" 40

Handout 5: "Role-Play 1: Diane/David" 41

Handout 6: "Role-Play 2: Jan" 42

Handout 7: "Role-Play 3: Les/Leslie" 43

Handout 8: "Role-Play 4: Robert/Roberta" 44

Handout 9: "Conflict Management Styles" 45

Handout 10: "Guidelines for Win/Win Conflict Resolution" 46

Handout 11: "Norman Cousins Quotation" 47

Evaluation 49

Sample Sessions from Other Volumes in the Series 51

Social Action Organizations and Resources for All Ages 63

Introduction to *In Our Hands*

"We, the member congregations of the Unitarian Universalist Association, covenant to affirm and promote: the inherent worth and dignity of every person; justice, equity, and compassion in human relations...."

So begins the Principles and Purposes covenant adopted by the Unitarian Universalist Association in 1985. The statement underscores the denomination's deep commitment to justice, a commitment that marks the history of the two liberal religious traditions, Unitarianism and Universalism.

Unitarian Universalists celebrate and remember a worthy collection of forebears who struggled for peace and justice. We remember Benjamin Rush and his timely defense of social equality in the late eighteenth century. We remember Theodore Parker's passion for abolition a generation later. We celebrate Adin Ballou's powerful critique of industrial society, Clara Barton, founder of the American Red Cross, and William Ellery Channing's abhorrence of poverty. We remember Dorothea Dix, reformer of prisons and psychiatric hospitals, and Susan B. Anthony, eminently successful suffragist. We honor Olympia Brown, Jane Addams, Elizabeth Blackwell, and Albert Schweitzer.

In more recent history, we celebrate the contributions of John Haynes Holmes, pacifist, human rights advocate, and co-founder of the War Resister's League and the American Civil Liberties Union. And Donald Thompson, shot as he stood up for civil rights in Jackson, Mississippi, in the early 1960s. We remember James Reeb, beaten to death for the same cause on the streets of Selma, Alabama, in 1965, and Whitney Young, Jr., head of the National Urban League. We celebrate, too, the Unitarian Universalist Association's decision to publish the controversial Pentagon Papers despite government harassment, and the Association's long-standing commitment to gay and lesbian civil rights.

We celebrated the fiftieth anniversary of the Unitarian Universalist Service Committee in 1989. The USC has worked at home to fund minority-directed community projects, and abroad to enable people to gain control over their political, economic, and social institutions. The UUSC has sponsored many fact-finding missions to Central America to publicize human rights violations. The UUSC has its roots in the Unitarian and Universalist service committees that aided World War II refugees and led humanitarian efforts throughout the world.

Grounded in this rich history, present-day Unitarian Universalists have a commitment to peace and justice that must look forward, not back. With the inspiration of such activists, we must live our lives as peacemakers and champions of fair play.

In Our Hands is a manifestation of our belief in ourselves, our children, and our future. The Peace and Social Justice Curriculum Team began its work in November 1983, and finished in November 1988. The team consisted primarily of Unitarian Universalists from the Pacific Northwest of the United States and British Columbia, Canada. The team developed five religious education curricula: programs for children from five to nine years old, from nine to twelve years, for junior-high age, for senior-high age, and for adults.

The team articulated the following statement, which has served as the philosophical center in the development of its curricula.

Peace and Social Justice Education for Unitarian Universalists: A Rationale

The Present Crisis

The most serious issues facing the world today are issues of peace and justice. The nuclear arms race, tyranny, hunger, poverty, torture, terrorism, even pollution and depletion of the world's resources are all problems of peace and justice. At the same time, although the magnitude and urgency of these problems is unprecedented in human history, issues of peace and justice have always been central concerns of human beings.

Linking Peace and Justice

Peace and justice are necessarily interdependent. Each requires the other. Real peace is not possible without justice. Injustice is the result of violence, which is often institutionalized as exploitation and oppression. Injustice is also a cause of violence in the form of criminal behavior, rebellion, and in reprisal, repression. In addition, true justice is not possible without peace. As long as individuals or groups are engaged in threats or acts of aggression, others are deprived of basic human rights, including freedom, equality, and life itself. Thus, peace and justice are both integral to the definition of the other. Peace is the achieving of justice, cooperation, and nonviolence. Justice is the realization of peace, freedom, and equality. Both peace and justice are necessary conditions for human fulfillment.

Ends and Means, Ideals and Realities

Peace and justice are at once ideal goals and actual processes. The vision of a just and peaceful world offers a stimulus for action and a standard by which to judge our efforts. As an actual process, however, peace and justice are always partial and never complete realizations of the ideal goal. Peace and justice are integral parts of the process by which the goals are sought. The means for achieving peace and justice must be congruent with the ends of peace and justice.

Moreover, even as ideal goals, peace and justice must not be viewed as states of perfect accord. A just and peaceful world will not be without disagreement and conflict or the exercise of power. The realization of peace and justice thus requires the nonviolent resolution of disagreement and conflict. It also requires an exercise of power by individuals and institutions that is characterized by and in the service of the ideals of peace and justice.

Cherishing the Earth

Peace and justice include an ecological dimension. The earth is our only source of material sustenance, as well as a major source of our spiritual nurturance. Degradation and destruction of the earth are inherently violent and lead to increasing conflict and injustice. Peace and justice require a reverence for the earth and an understanding of human interdependence, both material and spiritual, with the rest of nature.

Defining Peace and Justice

As an ideal goal, peace and justice are characterized by a set of relationships that describes both absence and presence:
- The *absence* of uncontrolled violence within the individual's psyche; and the *presence* of a sense of wholeness, self-worth, and empowerment within the individual's psyche; the acceptance of inner conflict and the ability to work with such conflict toward growth and integration.
- The *absence* of interpersonal violence; and the *presence* of interpersonal justice, in which justice is defined as fairness and respect due to each person by right and is based upon nonviolence, effective communication, conflict resolution, and cooperation; and the presence of basic political rights, such as freedom and equality, and basic social and economic rights, such as food, health care, employment, and education.
- The *absence* of violence among people of different nations, religions, and cultures; and the *presence* of justice among people of different nations, religions, and cultures, based upon nonviolence, effective communication, conflict resolution, and cooperation.
- The *absence* of destruction of the natural environment; and the *presence* of reverence for nature, and human behavior guided both by this reverence and by an understanding of our status as a part of nature and our interdependence with the rest of the natural world.

The ideal of peace and justice is dependent on four kinds of interrelated relationships:
- among the various parts of the individual's psyche (intrapersonal)
- between and among people (intrapersonal)
- between and among institutions of governance and religious faith (inter-institutional)
- between each individual and nature (global).

As we consider peace and justice as a process, not an ideal goal, we must see these characteristics not in terms of absolutes but in terms of their relative absence or presence.

Peace and Justice Education

The objective of peace and justice education is peace- and justice-making (or peace-making and justice-building). It engages people to stimulate and encourage their development as makers of peace and justice: within their own psyches, in their relationships with others, in their roles as citizens of a nation and members of a religious group, and in their identification as humans living on the earth.

Sources of Authority

Unitarian Universalists derive their authority for peace- and justice-making from several sources:

- their individual commitments to helping create peace and justice on this planet
- their reverence for life
- the Principles and Purposes of the Unitarian Universalist Association, adopted in 1985:
  We, the member congregations of the Unitarian Universalist Association, covenant to affirm and promote:

  - The inherent worth and dignity of every person
  - Justice, equity, and compassion in human relations
  - The right of conscience and the use of the democratic process within our congregations and in society at large
  - The goal of world community with peace, liberty, and justice for all
  - Respect for the interdependent web of all existence of which we are a part.

In Our Hands is a product of our history of commitment to peace and justice over the centuries, as exemplified by Unitarian Universalist heroines and heroes, including members of our own congregations and families; and our understanding and appreciation of the world's religions, all of which teach a version of "the golden rule."

Introduction to *Adults*

In Our Hands: Adults is a six-session program designed for groups of five to 15; 10 to 12 is optimum. Each session is planned for two hours.

The adult program involves participants in a collaborative inquiry into several central peace and justice issues: how we live with the nature of peace and justice in the world; how we bring peace and justice concerns into personal decisions; how we deal with interpersonal conflict; and how we envision a more peaceful and just world and choose to work toward making that vision a reality.

The adult program is based on the following set of assumptions:

Many Unitarian Universalist adults already possess considerable information about issues of peace and social justice and are wellinformed. However, information alone does not impel or equip people to explore issues of peace and justice that are interpersonal and intrapersonal. Exploring peace and justice issues on these levels requires introspection, increased self-awareness, and a willingness to interact and share oneself with others.

Information alone does not necessarily motivate people to work for peace and justice in their communities and in the larger world. In fact, information and an exclusive focus on the intellectual aspects of peace and justice issues can lead to feelings of hopelessness and despair and a state of resignation and inactivity. Unless people examine and work through their feelings, they are likely to become stuck either in the intensity of the feelings or in the effort to repress them. Either outcome makes people unable to act effectively for peace and justice in their lives.

Principles and Goals

The overall goal of *In Our Hands: Adults* is to engage participants in exploring their emotional, imaginative, and spiritual relationships with peace and justice issues within the context of constructive intellectual interaction. Such exploration can give people a more thorough intellectual understanding of peace and justice issues, a more profound understanding of their own emotional and spiritual relationship with peace and justice issues, and a deeper commitment to working for peace and justice within themselves, in their relationships with others, and in the larger world.

It is the intent of the program to help participants:

- Enlarge and sharpen felt awareness of peace and justice issues
- Explore the threats to the survival of humankind and other life on this planet and consider their feelings about these threats
- Explore the connections between peace and justice in their decision-making
- Explore the ways in which they deal with interpersonal conflict
- Explore the challenges of working to increase the quantity and quality of peace and justice in the world
- Choose to (re)commit themselves to working for peace and justice in the world and feel more empowered to do so.

Structure

Each session is organized as follows:

Gathering: Participants arrive, gather in a circle, and checkin.

Focusing: The main topic is introduced.

Reflecting: Participants react to the topic and express their feelings about and understanding of the topic.

Exploring: Participants explore the topic through interaction with new material and/or each other.

Integrating: Participants explore and share the

meaning of their activities in this session.

Closing: The session ends with a ritual closing.

Schedule

Options include:

- Hold a two-hour session once a week over a six-week period.
- Hold a two-day retreat, with six hours of program time each day.
- Hold a two-hour session each day for six days as part of a week-long summer conference or retreat.

Leaders

We strongly recommend a pair of co-leaders for this program. Co-leadership provides a richer experience for the participants by giving them two or more leaders with whom they can develop relationships.

Co-leadership also provides significant benefits for the leaders: Co-leaders don't feel isolated, because they are working with another person. They also can share with each other and give helpful feedback to each other. Through these interactions, the co-leaders can gain increasing competence and skill. They might also develop a friendship!

The leaders should participate in the activities of the program as much as possible. If there is only one leader, such participation will be limited. However, with a team of leaders, while one is leading, the other(s) can take part. This kind of participation strengthens the relationships between participants and leader(s) and removes the possible discomfort of having spectators in the room.

Guidelines for Openness and Sharing

There is much potential for open sharing throughout this program. On many occasions you will invite participants to share what may be intimate material. Therefore it is important that you let people know that you encourage them to speak only when they are comfortable; that it is always okay to pass if they choose not to share. Convey this message a few times in the beginning of the program to make sure that the participants take charge of their own sharing.

Be aware of the variety of experience that participants have in working with peace and justice issues and causes. People with different levels of experience bring different qualities, understanding, and feelings to the group. For example, those who are more experienced can be encouraged to share what they have learned with those who are less experienced. At the same time, those who are less experienced may have a freshness and enthusiasm that is valuable to those more experienced.

Environment

Arrange for a meeting area that is both comfortable and free of distractions and interruptions. The space should be clean, bright, and aesthetically pleasing.

Preparing to Lead

Here's one way to prepare to lead sessions:
1. Read over the session plan.
2. Then read the session plan again, jotting down the names of activities and brief descriptions on a notecard.
3. Do the preparation needed for the session.
4. Use the notecard you have prepared to guide you as you lead the session's activities.

Approximate Times

Each activity is accompanied by an approximate time, which is usually a range. These ranges are intended to give you information about how much time to allow for the the various activities. Of course, the time required to complete any particular activity can vary considerably depending on group size, the characteristics of the group, and leadership style.

Be aware that the approximate times are suggestions and approximations, not requirements or limitations. Be responsive to the energies of the group as they engage in each activity. At the same time, lead your group through a session plan in such a way that each activity receives appropriate attention.

Checking-In

At the beginning of Sessions 2 through 6, you will engage participants in a brief checking-in activity. A checking-in is an opportunity for people to share something that is going on in their lives: experiences during the past week, high points and low ones, ideas and feelings that are salient for them now, and so on. We suggest that you ask participants to checkin or share while keeping in mind the themes of this program—peace and social justice. Ask them to reflect on their thoughts, feelings, and experiences of the past week that relate to peace and justice, and to voice their reflections if they wish.

Model a checking-in process that is open and sharing, but also relatively brief.

Optional Passages for Focusing

Each session includes a Focusing activity. Sessions 1 and 6 use a quote from Norman Cousins as part of this activity. Session 2 uses a collection of quotation and/or pictures. Sessions 3, 4, and 5 let you decide if you want to use a quotation or passage as an element in Focusing. Be responsive to the wishes of the group in this decision.

A collection of passages is included at the end of the session plans. Also feel free to use an appropriate passage of your own selection. Your congregation's library is probably an excellent place to start looking.

Breaks

Each session calls for a 10-minute break roughly in the middle of the two hours. Note that while each break is listed under a particular activity, for example, Reflecting or Exploring, the time for the break is not included in the suggested time for that activity.

Closing

The Closing in each session calls for the group to end with the lighting of the chalice, some time for silent reflection, and a variety of other elements. The goal of this activity is to invite people to share a common ritual, during which they can reflect on the understanding they have developed during the previous two hours and reinforce their feelings of connection and cohesion with each other.

Using the "Reflection and Planning" Questions

At the end of each session plan is a section titled "Reflection and Planning." The questions are designed to guide your reflection about and evaluation of that session. We strongly suggest that you take the time each week both to consider these questions yourself and to discuss them with your co-leader.

Your deliberate evaluation of your own leadership experience is the best way for you to recognize your strengths and weaknesses as a group leader and, working from this recognition, to grow as a leader. Your co-leader can provide you with information about your behavior that you do not perceive, and you can provide similar constructive feedback to her or him. Even five minutes of reflection and discussion after each session can make a significant contribution to your growth and effectiveness as a leader.

Social Time

Each session plan suggests that you arrange for a social time after Closing. This time gives participants an opportunity to process the events of the session in an informal way, as well as get to know each other better. Plan to bring refreshments for the social time at the end of Session 1, then recruit volunteers to bring refreshments for the other sessions. For the final session, you may want to arrange for more elaborate refreshments. Discuss with the participants what they would like to do for this occasion.

Leading Guided Imagery and Meditation

Several sessions include guided imagery or guided meditation. These activities are particularly helpful in bringing intuitive knowledge to the conscious level. Intuition, by definition, is knowledge that resides in the unconscious and that comes to consciousness directly, without the mediation of reason. Guided imagery and meditation are processes that can help people gain access to their imaginative and intuitive potential and generate new and innovative patterns, hypotheses, and conceptions.

If you have not led this kind of activity before, practice a few times with family or friends before you lead it for your group.

When leading guided imagery or meditation, speak clearly yet soothingly; softly, yet strongly enough for everyone to hear you. Try to arrange your space to be quiet and darkened, and without interruptions as you lead these activities. If possible, have a room with a rug that people can lie on.

Begin each guided imagery or meditation by asking people to find a comfortable place to lie down on their backs. (People who choose not to lie down can sit comfortably with their spines straight on a straight-backed chair or against a wall.) Ask them to let themselves find a comfortable position and to close their eyes. Then say something like:

"Take deep, slow breaths, and listen to your body breathing... (Each set ellipses directs you to pause for about five seconds.) Breathe deeply, in and out, in and out... Now tense every muscle in your body when I say 'hold' and then let go when I say 'release.' Okay, hold—release... One more time, hold—release. Now feel relaxation down in your feet... Feel a wave of relaxation moving up into your legs... Up into your calves... And up into your thighs... Now feel the relaxation moving up into your pelvic region... Now moving up through your stomach... And your chest... And now flowing up along your back... Now feel the relaxation in your hands... Feel it moving up your arms... And into your shoulders... And up your neck... Feel your jaw relaxing... And now feel the relaxation in your face... And now feel the relaxation gathering in the crown of your head... And now you are totally relaxed. Lie quietly for a little bit, and let your mind empty itself of its busyness. And continue to feel yourself breathe..."

Allow about 30 seconds of silence, then begin the guided imagery or meditation.

Be aware that a significant percentage of adults do not see clear pictures in their imaginations. Most do, however, experience other kinds of "imagery" in this activity: for example, feelings, sounds, body sensations, and ideas. Prior to the first guided imagery activity, ask participants not to have any specific expectations of this process but simply to be open and pay attention to whatever comes into their awareness. Explain that in this context, imagery includes pictures, feelings, sounds, body sensations, ideas, and so on, and that whatever comes into consciousness is usually related to the experience of the imagery or meditation and is worthy of attention.

Session 1 ♦ Orientation and Beginnings

Goals for Participants

- to gain an appreciation of one another and this program
- to begin to develop trust within this group
- to affirm publicly one or more personal convictions about peace and justice and to reflect on this affirmation through discussion
- to explore their expectations for this program and share those expectations with one another
- to examine the principles of the Unitarian Universalist Association with respect to peace and justice issues.

Overview

This session engages participants in exploring peace and justice issues on intellectual, emotional, and spiritual levels. Each participant is invited to enter into this collaborative inquiry as a whole person.

The activities also begin to build a group environment in which people can feel respected and supported. A trusting and nurturing interpersonal environment is essential if participants are to explore issues of peace and justice in a meaningful and open way.

Materials

- Nametags
- Newsprint, markers, tape, and easel
- A manila folder with a few sheets of paper for each participant
- Pens or pencils
- A copy of Handout 1 ("Program Outline"), Handout 2 ("Program Goals"), and Handout 3 ("Unitarian Universalist Principles") for each participant
- Refreshments for a social time after the session
- A chalice, candle, and matches

Preparation

- Set up a circle of chairs.
- Set up the easel and newsprint.
- Make newsprint-sized posters of Handouts 1 and 2 and the following six questions:

    1. Which expression was easier, yes or no?
    2. Is it more fun to say no or yes?
    3. Which expression held more feeling for you?
    4. Which is easier to identify—what we don't want or what we do want?
    5. What do I feel about this experience now?
    6. What did I learn from this experience?

- Print the following quotation from Norman Cousins on a sheet of newsprint:

The starting point for a better world is the belief that it is possible. Civilization begins in the imagination. The wild dream is the first step to reality. It is the direction finder by which people locate higher goals and discern their highest selves.
—Norman Cousins

- Choose an appropriate place for posting the several newsprint-sized posters.

- Bring refreshments for a group social time after the session. At the end of this and following sessions, elicit volunteers to bring the re-freshments for the next session.

Session Plan

Gathering 15-30 minutes

Make a nametag and put it on. Greet the participants individually as they arrive. Introduce yourself to anyone whom you do not know. Make the nametags and markers available, and ask each person to make and wear a nametag.

When the group has gathered, ask people to join you in the circle. Introduce yourself and welcome the participants to this program.

Explain that you are going to ask them to introduce themselves to the group by sharing their names and something about what has motivated them to take part in this program. You may want to go first by sharing what has motivated you to lead this program. Or elicit a volunteer to go first and then go around the circle from that person. If you do the latter, be sure to share your motivation when your turn comes.

When all of the participants have introduced themselves, tell people that you'd like them to share again by briefly relating one experience they have had, as a participant or a witness, in which a wrong was righted or a conflict was resolved successfully. Elicit a volunteer to go first, and go around the circle in the opposite direction from the introduction circle.

Focusing 8-10 minutes

Hand out the folders and make the pens or pencils available. Invite participants to keep all of the handouts they receive and their own writings from this program in their folders.

Post the Norman Cousins passage and invite the group to reflect on it for a little while. Then ask people to share how this statement feels to them. Tell them that you would like this expression to be a sharing, not a discussion or debate. Note that if people want to discuss, they can do so later. Then allow all who wish to share to do so.

Reflecting 25-40 minutes

Tell the participants that you are going to engage them in an activity called "Saying No and Saying Yes." Introduce it by saying something like:

"There are times in our lives, often times of great threat, of intense crisis, of powerful joy, when it becomes startlingly clear what we must say no to and what we want to affirm in our lives—to say yes to. Over the course of human history, we as a species have sometimes made significant gains by saying no. For example, we have said no to cannibalism. On the whole, we have said no to incest. And we have said no to slavery. This activity is about the experience of saying no and saying yes."

Ask people to stand. Then go on:

"Now let's practice saying no together. On the count of three, I want you to say no and to mean it. One... two... three!"

Have the group say no a couple of times. Invite them to put genuine feeling into their expression. Then go on:

"Now I want you to put your whole body into your no. As you say no, move your body in whatever way expresses that feeling. Okay? One... two... three!"

Have the group repeat this once or twice more. Again encourage people to be expressive. Then say something like:

"Now that we've worked with what it feels like to say no, let's join that feeling with some specific idea or value. Let me demonstrate."

Pick something that you say no to personally—for example, war toys—and say, with all the intensity of your feeling into your statement: "I say no to war toys."

Once you have modeled this process, elicit volunteers to share in the same way. After a few people have done so, interject that you'd like to add one other element to this experience. Ask all those who agree with what each speaker has said to punctuate her or his statement with a chorus of no's. Clarify this by giving an example: The speaker says, "I say no to nuclear war." And those who agree, as a chorus, say, "No!"

Once everyone understands the procedure, invite people to resume offering statements that say no.

Note: If you are uncomfortable with the group dynamics of such an activity or the possibility of group pressure being exerted on individuals in an undesirable way, you may want to omit the chorus.

When all who wish to have shared their no statements, and you have invited people to share more than once if they like, follow the same procedure with saying yes.

When the group has gone through all of the steps in the procedure with yes, ask people to sit down again in a circle. Post the sheet of newsprint you have prepared with the six questions. Lead the group in a discussion of their experiences with and reactions to the yes-and-no activity. Use the questions as a guide for your discussion to the extent that they are helpful.

When you have reached the end of this discussion, take a 10-minute break.

Exploring 35-45 minutes

Gather the group in a circle. Give people a few minutes to reflect on their expectations for this program and to jot down several of these expectations on a sheet of paper.

When participants have finished writing, ask them to organize themselves into groups of four or five. Have them move their chairs so the small-group members sit together. Elicit a volunteer from each group to act as a recorder. Then ask people to share the expectations they have noted with each other. As they share, ask them to be aware of expectations that are cited by several people in the group. Ask the recorder to keep track of such mutual expectations and be prepared to share them with the whole group.

After six to eight minutes, gather the whole group back in a circle. Have the recorders read their lists of common expectations. Invite reactions.

Display the posters of Handouts 1 and 2, which you have prepared on newsprint. Ask people to read these, and invite discussion. If there are significant expectations of this program that will not be addressed by the curriculum, raise this with the group, either now or later on, and decide if and how you want to add to or modify the program to meet these expectations.

When the discussion has come to an end, distribute copies of Handouts 1 and 2, and invite people to keep them in their folders.

Distribute Handout 3. Ask people to return to their small groups, and read the Purposes and Principles. Then write the questions below on a sheet of newsprint, and ask people to discuss their responses to these questions in their small groups:

- What personal relationship do you experience to these principles?

- Why is it that most of the seven principles of the UUA speak to peace and justice concerns?

- How do you feel about this?

When time requires, gather everyone in a circle. Invite people to characterize briefly the nature of their small-group discussions.

Integrating 10-15 minutes

Tell the group that you are going to involve them in a short guided meditation. Ask them to sit comfortably and to close their eyes until you ask them to open them. Then ask people to take a couple of long, slow, deep breaths. Go on to lead the meditation by saying something like the following. (Remember that each set of ellipses—three periods in a row—means to pause for five seconds.)

"As you breathe out, feel tension flowing out of your body... And as you breathe in, feel energy coming in. Now breathe out, and feel tension flowing away from you... And now breathe in, and feel calming energy flowing into your body... Now breathe out, and feel any tenseness going away... And now breathe in, and feel yourself more and more relaxed... And now breathe out... Now breathe in... Breathe out... And breathe in... And now feel yourself very calm, relaxed, very much at ease and still very aware." (Pause for ten seconds.) "Now let your whole self listen to the words of this prayer." (Read aloud the following prayer.)

> Hear O Humankind, the prayer of my heart.
> Are we not one?
> Have we not one desire,
> to heal our Mother Earth,
> to bind her wounds?
>
> Are we not all brothers and sisters?
> Are we not all grandchildren of the same
>   mystery?
> Do we not all want to love and be loved?
> Do we not want to work and play and sing
> and dance together?
>
> Hear my heart's prayer, O Humankind!
> Life is the only treasure,
> we are custodians of it.
> It is our sacred trust.
> Life is wondrous, awesome, and holy.
> Life is burning glory
> And its price is simply this: Courage.
>
> We must be brave enough to love.
>
> —Manitonquat

Allow a minute of silence when you have finished reading. Then ask people to open their eyes. Gather the group in your circle, and invite people to share their reactions to this prayer. Help them to stay with sharing reactions, not debating or even discussing.

Closing 5-7 minutes

Remind people of your next meeting date and time, and give them a brief preview of the next session.

Place the chalice in the center of the circle, and light it. Then say something like:

"This chalice light is one of our Unitarian Universalist symbols of clarity, of elemental connection, of hope. Let me ask you all to share one hope you hold concerning the state of peace and justice on our planet."

Find a volunteer to begin, and then go around the circle, asking those who wish to share to do so.

When all have shared who wish to, ask the participants to join you in a few moments of silence to reflect upon what people have expressed. Then extinguish the candle, and invite people to the social time. If desired, collect the nametags so they can be used at the next session.

Reflection and Planning

Consider these questions, and discuss them with your co-leader(s):

1. How do I feel about this session now?

2. If I were to lead this session again, what would I do differently?

3. What preparation do I need to do for the next session?

Session 2 ♦ What Is the State of Peace and Justice in the World?

Goals for Participants

- to continue to get to know one another
- to increase the sense of trust and safety in the group
- to explore their understandings and feelings, and those of their peers, about the state of peace and justice in the world
- to enlarge and sharpen their awareness of peace and justice issues
- to evaluate their personal relationship to the issues of peace and justice.

Overview

In this session, participants explore their feelings and their understandings about the state of peace and justice in the world through a consideration of both the "good news" and the "bad news" of peace and justice. They also explore their own relationship to peace and justice issues to better understand this relationship.

The focus in this session flows from a broad survey of peace and justice issues in the world to the more particular concern of how participants participate in and experience these issues. Participants are invited to explore their connection to these issues at whatever level of depth and intensity they choose.

Materials

- Newsprint, markers, tape, and easel
- A selection of pictures and/or quotations, as described in Preparation
- A tape player and a tape of calm, reflective music
- Paper, pens, and pencils
- Copies of Handout 4 ("Guidelines for Your Peace and Justice Story")
- Nametags from Session 1 or nametag supplies
- Refreshments for social time
- Chalice, candle, and matches

Preparation

- Set up your usual circle and easel.
- Have the tape player and music ready for use.
- Have available for each participant a picture or quotations (or both) that raises a peace and justice issue. Include pictures and/or quotation that express both the "bad news" and the "good news" about peace and justice; for example: pictures of hunger, poverty, lack of shelter, combat, and so on; pictures of people caring for others, people collaborating, scenes of natural beauty. Some sources for pictures are *National Geographic* and various news magazines. Look for age, gender, and racial inclusiveness.

Here are some examples of quotations:

Some 40,000 children die daily from conditions related to poverty and malnutrition.
—UNICEF

Today the real test of power is not the capacity to make war, but the capacity to prevent it.
—Anne O'Hare McCormick

There is no way to peace, peace is the way.
—A.J. Muste

[In 1986] world military expenditures [were] running at an historic high of $1.7 million a minute — $770 billion a year [in 1983 dollars].
—Ruth Sivard

Other quotations can be found on pages 172-175 of *Peace Experiments*, a program published by the Unitarian Universalist Peace Network and available through the UUA Bookstore.

Session Plan

Gathering — 8-12 minutes

Greet participants individually as they arrive. If desired, have them make nametags, or reuse the ones from the previous session.

When the group has gathered, ask people to join you in a circle. Introduce the idea of checking-in as described in the Introduction. Then engage the group in a brief checking-in, focusing on their thoughts and feelings about peace and justice during the past week.

Focusing — 8-12 minutes

After the checking-in, give people a brief overview of this session. Explain that you are going to give each person a picture or quotation (or both), and ask them to consider their picture or quotation and reflect on its meanings for a few minutes. Play the reflective piece of music, and hand out a picture or quotation (or both) to each participant.

Allow two or three minutes for reflection. Then turn off the music, and invite participants to show their picture or read their quotation to the group and to convey briefly what this picture or quotation means to them. Elicit volunteers to share, or go around the circle, asking for responses.

Reflecting — 30-45 minutes

Begin this activity by saying something like:

"To explore the issues of peace and justice in the world, we must be truly willing to open ourselves to naming the whole range of realities and possibilities: that which we find heartening and hopeful, that which we dislike and deplore, that which we can support and work for, and that which disgusts and terrifies us. One way to think of all of this is to think in terms of the 'good news' and the 'bad news.'"

Explain that the group will now explore these two categories, starting with the good news. Ask people to share their views about the good news by completing sentences like:

- I am most encouraged by...

- I feel good about...

- I feel hopeful about...

- Something important for me is...

You may want to write these incomplete sentences on a sheet of newsprint. Elicit sharing from participants either by asking for volunteers or by going around the circle. Ask people to share only one statement at a time, but invite them to share more statements during the course of this activity.

When the group has exhausted the good news, follow the same procedure with the bad news. Use incomplete sentences like the following:

- I am most discouraged by...

- I am unhappy or angry about...

- I feel threatened by...

- Something important for me is...

When the group has exhausted the bad news, invite members to share their reactions to this experience. After some participants have shared on their own initiative, raise questions like:

- When you consider the good news and the bad news together, what do you see as the whole picture?

- How do you feel when you look at both the bad news and the good news together?

When the group has discussed these questions, take a 10-minute break.

Exploring — 40-45 minutes

Ask participants to organize themselves into groups of three. If you have co-leaders, one can participate while the other keeps track of the time. Tell people they will have an opportunity to tell their peace and justice stories to the other members of their group. Distribute copies of Handout 4 and go over the guidelines with the group. Invite questions about the guidelines, and respond to any.

Tell people that they will each have ten minutes to tell their story and that you will let them know both when eight minutes have elapsed and when it is time to conclude.

Ask for a volunteer in each group to begin. Remember to announce the eight- and ten-minute time marks during the activity.

When everyone has told her or his story, invite the group members to share in their groups their reactions to each others' stories. Note that they will have only five minutes for this.

After five minutes, gather the whole group together. Ask each participant to share one feeling she or he has after hearing and telling the peace and justice stories. Ask them to limit their expression to a sentence or two. Go around the circle, inviting participation.

Integrating 10-12 minutes

Tell the group that you are going to lead them through a short guided imagery. Ask people to find comfortable positions, sitting or lying on their backs, and to close their eyes. Then lead the guided imagery by saying something like:

"Now I'd like you to relax and take a couple of deep breaths. And when you breathe out, imagine tension flowing out and away from your body and mind. And when you breathe in, imagine new, calm energy flowing into your body and mind. Okay, now breathe out slowly and easily... And now breathe in, evenly and deeply... And now breathe out... And now breathe in... And breathe out... And breathe in... And now let your breathing go along on its own..." (Pause for 10 seconds.)

"Now when I say so, I'd like you to tense the muscles in your feet and legs, hold them tense for a few seconds, and let them go. Okay, tense them... And let them go. And feel the relaxation now from your feet up through your legs... Now tense your stomach muscles, and hold them... And let them go... And now tense your chest muscles, and hold them... Now let them go... And now your back muscles... And let them go... And now tense your hands, your arms, and your shoulders... And hold them... And let them go... Now feel the relaxation all the way from your feet to your shoulders... And let that wave of relaxation move up into your neck... Into your jaw... Into all of your face... Into all of your head." (Pause for 10 seconds.)

"Now that you are relaxed, I'd like you to imagine that you are walking on a bare, rocky hillside. You are walking up the incline, toward a group of large, jagged rocks that you can see in the distance... Now you are walking along purposefully, making good time as you climb the hill. You know that behind those rocks, you will meet someone who will be a teacher for you... Now you are still climbing up, moving easily... You are nearing the rocks, and you slow down... For a moment you wonder if you want to go on, if you really want to know what you will hear from this teacher. And then at once, you answer your own question. Yes!... Your teacher will tell you something about your own peace and justice story. Now you stand right next to the rocks. I'd like you to walk around them and find out what your teacher has to tell you about your peace and justice story." (Pause for one to two minutes.)

"Now it is time for you to leave your teacher and begin your return. So thank your teacher and say goodbye... And now come out from behind the rocks, and begin to walk down the rocky hill... You are moving down quickly, lightly... Moving down almost like gliding... And now you are almost down... And now you have returned to where you began. When you are ready, I'd like you to return to this room and open your eyes. But please remain silent when you do this."

Closing 5-8 minutes

When all participants have opened their eyes, ask them to remain silent and return to the circle. Place the chalice in the center of the circle, and light it. Then say something like:

"Our Unitarian Universalist chalice can remind us of the value of insight – to see the truth within. In this special place of our closing, I'd like to invite each of you to share something about what you learned from your inner teacher."

Elicit volunteers. When all have shared who wish to, ask people to join you in a few minutes of silent reflection.

Then give people a brief overview of the next session. Invite people to the social time, and collect the nametags if you wish to use them again.

Reflection and Planning

Consider the questions below, and discuss them with your co-leader(s):

1. What was the best part of this session? Why?

2. What did I like the least? Why?

3. What did I learn from the experience of leading this session?

4. What preparation do I need to do for the next session?

Session 3 ♦ Do We Choose Peace and Justice?

Goals for Participants

- to continue to get to know one another
- to develop a sense of trust and safety in the group
- to explore their decision-making experiences in relation to personal and interpersonal peace and justice
- to become more aware of how they make decisions relating to peace and justice in their lives
- to consider the ways in which peace-making and justice-building can both enhance and diminish one another in their own lives.

Overview

In this session, participants explore how their own decision-making both fosters and hinders the peaceful and just qualities of their lives. As a part of this exploration, participants consider how they treat themselves and others when decisions involve peace and justice issues.

An important concern of this session is the interaction between peace-making and justice-building. There are times when actions for peace can diminish the quality of justice that exists in a situation. For example, if you placate the other person in a conflict, you may enhance peace at the expense of the justice that you receive. The inverse is also possible and probably equally common. However, peace and justice can also interact in such a way that the establishment of one supports the other, or even generates the other. It is important to explore this range of potential in the relationship between peace and justice, and examine what kinds of actions can make peace and build justice synergistically.

Materials

- Newsprint, markers, tape, and easel
- Unlined white paper
- Many different-colored markers and crayons
- Refreshments for social time
- Chalice, candle, and matches

Preparation

- Set up your usual circle and easel.

- Choose a selection from Optional Passages to use in Focusing (if desired).

- Have work tables available for the activity in Reflecting.

- Print on newsprint the five decision questions in Exploring, but do not post until that time.

Session Plan

Gathering 6-12 minutes

Greet participants individually as they arrive. You may want to use the nametags for one more session.

When the group has gathered, ask people to join you in a circle. Engage people in a brief checking-in, as described in the Introduction.

Focusing 3-6 minutes

Say something like:
"Today we are going to explore what peace means to us, what justice means, and how the two interrelate as we make decisions."

Then give a brief overview of the session.

If desired, read aloud a passage that you have selected for Focusing. Invite brief responses.

Reflecting   20-30 minutes

Give each participant a sheet of white paper. Make the crayons and markers available. Ask people to draw an image that depicts or expresses peace for them. Note that they do not need to be concerned about the skill of their drawing; what is important is that the image they create be evocative for them personally.

Allow five or six minutes for drawing, or more if people want more time. Then ask people to find a partner, show their image to their partner, and explain why this image evokes peace for them.

Give people about five minutes for discussion. While they are talking, give each pair a sheet of newsprint.

After about five minutes, ask participants to work with their partners to create an image that depicts or expresses justice. They should use the sheet of newsprint for this drawing.

Allow five or six minutes for drawing, or more if people want more time. Then gather the group, and elicit volunteer pairs to show their images to the group and explain them briefly.

When all have shared who wish to do so, bring this activity to a close by offering some appropriate generalizations about the images of peace and justice that the members of the group have created.

Depending on how much time you have allowed for Reflecting, take a 10-minute break before or after Exploring.

Exploring   20-30 minutes

Tell participants that you are going to lead them through a kind of guided remembrance. Invite people to find a comfortable position, close their eyes, and relax. Ask them to take several deep breaths, feeling tension flow away from their body and mind as they breathe out, and feeling energy flow in as they breathe in.

Give participants about 30 seconds to breathe in this way, and then say something like:

"Now I would like you to recall a difficult decision you have had to make sometime in the last year, or the last couple of years. Let yourself consider which decision you want to explore now." (Pause for 15 seconds.)

"Now that you have chosen a decision, I want you to get inside of the situation that led to that decision. What was going on?" (Pause for 20 seconds.)

"What were your options? What seemed to be the consequences of each option? And how did you feel about these options?" (Pause for 20 seconds.)

"Now I would like you to recall your decision-making process. How did you decide? What was your decision? And why?" (Pause for 20 seconds.)

"And now I would like you to hold on to as much of that experience as you can and, when you are ready, come back to this room and open your eyes. Please keep silent while you do this."

When all participants have "returned," ask people to organize themselves into groups of three. Post the newsprint with the questions below and invite each person to take a few minutes to share their responses in their small group.

- What was the situation that you recalled?

- What decision did you make?

- Why did you make the decision you did?

- Did that decision lead to peace for yourself?

- Did that decision lead to justice for yourself?

As participants are sharing, print the following questions on a sheet of newsprint:

- How does peace-making affect the quality of justice in a decision?

- How does justice-building affect the quality of peace in a decision?

As the small groups near the end of their sharing, post the second set of questions, and invite participants to consider and discuss these questions as well.

When all of the small groups have had five or six minutes to discuss the second set of questions, gather all participants into a circle. Ask people to share conclusions or generalizations they have articulated in their small groups. Invite discussion.

Integrating   25 minutes

Ask participants to return to the same small groups. Then ask people either to think of a difficult decision they are facing now, or to return to the decision they considered previously, and to try to articulate a decision that would foster both peace and justice. Ask them to discuss this with the other members of their small group and to call on these members for help. Note that each person will have six minutes.

Invite people to begin. Remember to note each of the six-minute intervals.

When each participant has discussed her or his decision, gather the whole group. Invite discussion by asking questions like the following:

- What is your belief now about the ways in which peace-making and justice-building interact in decisions like the ones we have just explored?

- Are there ways to foster both peace and justice in our personal and interpersonal lives?

Closing   3-5 minutes

When time requires, call the discussion to a halt. Give people a brief preview of the next session.

Place the chalice in the center of the circle, and light it. Say something like:

"Let us look into the light now, and consider how peace must be part of the fabric of justice, and how justice must be part of the fabric of peace."

Allow a minute of silence. Then extinguish the candle, and invite people to the social time.

Reflection and Planning

Consider the questions below, and discuss them with your co-leader(s):

1. How do I feel about the people in this group now?

2. What did I learn from leading this session?

3. What preparations do I need to do for the next session?

Session 4 ♦ How Do We Live a Just and Peaceful Life with Others?

Goals for Participants

- to consider the nature of conflict in interpersonal relationships
- to examine their own style(s) of conflict management
- to explore a method for constructive conflict resolution and to consider its value as a tool for promoting peace and justice in interpersonal relations.

Overview

In this session, participants explore the nature of conflict in interpersonal relationships and examine a method for creative conflict resolution, the win/win rules. Participants are also invited to consider their own conflict management style(s) and to apply the win/win rules to a real conflict in their lives.

Materials

- Newsprint, markers, tape, and easel
- Cardboard and string for small signs
- Copies of Handout 5 ("Role-Play 1") and Handout 6 ("Role-Play 2"), depending on the option you choose in Exploring
- If desired, copies of Handout 7 ("Role-Play 3") and Handout 8 ("Role-Play 4")
- Copies of Handout 9 ("Conflict Management Styles") and Handout 10 ("Guidelines for Win/Win Conflict Resolution") for all participants
- Refreshments for social time
- Chalice, candle, and matches

Preparation

- Set up your usual circle and easel.
- Choose a selection from Optional Passages to use in Focusing (if desired)
- Make copies of the role-play parts.
- Photocopy Handouts 9 and 10 for all participants.
- Make a newsprint-sized poster of the Seeds Chart (from Focusing).
- Make two small signs that can be worn with string around the neck or pinned on: one saying Jan, the other saying Diane or David.

Session Plan

Gathering   6-12 minutes

Greet participants individually as they arrive. When the group has gathered, ask people to join you in a circle. Engage participants in a brief checking-in.

Focusing   20-30 minutes

Introduce participants to the topic of this session, and give them a brief overview of the session plan.

If desired, read aloud a passage you have chosen. Then invite brief responses.

Tell people that the group will begin to work with the issue of peace and justice in interpersonal relationships through a role-play. When two people have volunteered, give each of them one of the role-play parts.

Give the volunteers a minute to consider their parts. While they are doing this, set the scene for the rest of the group. Have each role-player wear her or his name sign. Then ask the role-players to begin.

Please note that the role-play situation is designed to generate conflict. If the role-players resolve the conflict constructively, adapt the session plan to that outcome.

You will decide when to stop the role-play. Allow it to play out enough so that the conflict has a good amount of development. When you do stop the role-play, invite each role-player to share a little about how she or he feels now from the perspective of her or his character. When both people have shared, thank them for volunteering and ask them to return to the group.

Display a chart like the Seeds Chart (below) on the easel. Ask people to recall the role-play they have just seen and to offer suggestions for both categories on the chart. List the suggestions in the appropriate column. When the group has run out of suggestions, ask people to examine the chart as a whole. Invite reactions to it. Then ask the following questions and elicit brief responses:

- What style of managing this conflict has each character used?

- Do you think that this conflict can be resolved constructively?

Reflecting 18-25 minutes

Ask participants to organize into pairs and sit with their partners. Then say something like:

"I would like you to think of a conflict you have taken part in recently. I'll give you some time to choose one." (Pause for 10 seconds.)

"I would like you to envision this situation clearly in your mind." (Pause for 10 seconds.)

"Now I would like you to determine what style you used to deal with or manage this conflict. By style I mean your approach to it. For example, did you try to avoid it? To win? To compromise? How did you go about dealing with it?" (Pause for 10 seconds.)

"Now please ask yourself: Is the style of managing conflict that I used in this one situation characteristic of the way that I usually manage conflict? Reflect on this question for a bit." (Pause for 20 seconds.)

"Now I would like you to share with your partner whatever conclusions you have drawn about your most commonly used style (or styles) of conflict management."

Give participants five to eight minutes to talk. Then gather them in a circle, and distribute copies of Handout 9. Go over the chart quickly, and invite discussion.

Seeds of Peace/Justice	**Seeds of Conflict**

The value implications of this chart are likely to arise during this discussion. In other words, participants will probably conclude that problem-solving is the best way to resolve conflict. (If participants don't raise this issue, raise it yourself.) Note that the group will explore the nature of problem-solving and its uses and limitations in the next activity.

At the end of the discussion, take a 10-minute break.

Exploring 30-40 minutes

Begin this activity by saying something like:

"The problem-solving style of managing conflict may not be useful for all conflicts, because it requires that both parties enter into the process of resolution without holding onto the goal of making the other party lose. Yet this style or approach may be more useful than you think, particularly if you know and can apply the steps in the process."

Distribute copies of Handout 10, and ask people to examine the guidelines. When they have done so, invite questions and comments. Encourage appropriate discussion.

After a suitable amount of time, continue with one of the three options described below.

Option 1

Explain that you would like to try the role-play again, seeing if the win/win rules can be applied. Elicit four volunteers. Note that two of them will play the roles and the other two will act as process guides, with one guide assigned to each role-player. Have people volunteer for which role they want to enact.

Give the parts to the role-players and allow them a minute to read their parts. Then assign a process guide to each role-player. Explain that the task of the process guide is to help her or his role-player enact the win/win rules. To communicate with her or his role-player, a guide should say, "Freeze!" This command stops the action for a minute while the role-player and guide converse.

Be sure that all players understand their tasks. Then have the role-play begin.

When the role-play has reached a conclusion (or when you stop it because of time constraints), ask the role-players and the guides to share a little about their experiences in the role-play. Then invite discussion from the rest of the group.

Option 2

Follow the same procedure as Option 1, using Role-Plays 3 and 4 instead of 1 and 2.

Option 3

Have the group discuss how they might apply the win/win rules to the conflict in the role-play they have already enacted/observed in Focusing, without re-enacting the role-play.

Integrating 10-20 minutes

Ask participants to re-form the pairs that they created earlier in the session, or have them form new pairs. Ask the partners to interact in the following way:

1. Partner A describes a real conflict that she or he is experiencing now, has experienced recently, or expects to experience soon.

2. Partner A explores how she or he might apply the win/win rules to resolving this conflict constructively.

3. Partner B listens carefully and helps by asking questions and offering suggestions.

4. The partners switch roles, and go through the process again.

Let people know when it is almost halfway through the time for this activity, when it is exactly halfway, when it is almost time to finish, and when it is time to stop.

Have the pairs begin. Remember to announce the time marks.

Closing 5-7 minutes

Gather the group in the circle. Give participants a brief preview of the next session. Then place the chalice in the center of the circle and light it. Invite people to share one reaction they have to the win/win rules.

When all have shared who wish to, allow a few moments of silence. Then extinguish the candle. Invite people to the social time.

Reflection and Planning

Consider the questions below, and discuss them with your co-leader(s):

1. What was the best part of this session? Why?

2. What did I like least about this session? Why?

3. If I were to lead this session again, what would I do differently?

4. What preparation do I need to do for the next session?

Session 5 ♦ What Are Our Visions of a Just and Peaceful World?

Goals for Participants

- to discover and share their visions of a more just and peaceful world
- to identify the obstacles to progressing toward peace and justice
- to explore the most powerful methods for achieving greater peace and justice.

Overview

In this session, participants reflect on and articulate some of their own visions of what would make a more peaceful and just world and how we might move toward that world. Each participant's vision will inevitably be incomplete. They will find, however, that the process of sharing many visions will bring a fullness to the articulation of a more just and peaceful world; the whole is likely to exceed the sum of the parts.

Encourage participants to be guided by their values and at the same time to be as concrete and realistic as possible in their visioning. You may want to acknowledge that this is a somewhat paradoxical instruction.

Materials

- Newsprint, markers, tape, and easel
- Writing paper
- Pens or pencils
- Six stick-on stars for each participant
- Tape player
- Calm, meditative, yet energetic music on tape
- If you choose Option 2 in Integrating: several large sheets of oaktag for the collages; several pairs of scissors; tape or glue; markers; magazines from which pictures may be cut; and other appropriate collage materials
- Refreshments for social time
- Chalice, candle, and matches

Preparation

- Set up your usual circle and easel.

- Have tape player and music ready for use. The music should be at least five minutes long. The Windham Hill label carries appropriate calm, meditative, energetic music.

- Choose a selection from Optional Passages to use in Focusing (if desired).

- Prepare the posters of the questions for Exploring by printing each of the questions below at the top of its own sheet of newsprint:

  – What are the five most pressing needs in our search for a more peaceful and just world?
  – What are the five most powerful obstacles to our progress toward a more peaceful and just world?
  – What are the five most powerful methods for achieving a more peaceful and just world?

Session Plan

Gathering   6-12 minutes

Greet participants individually as they arrive. When the group has gathered, ask people to join you in a circle. Engage people in a brief checking-in.

Focusing   2-6 minutes

Give participants a brief overview of the session. Distribute the writing paper and pens or pencils.
   If desired, read aloud the passage that you have chosen. Invite responses.

Reflecting 30-35 minutes

Tell participants that you are going to play a piece of music and that while it plays, you would like them to envision what the world could be like in 25 years if things go well and the world becomes a more peaceful and just place. Encourage people to be both imaginative and realistic. Note the paradoxical quality of this request if that seems helpful.

Ask people to just reflect for a few moments, and then to write some notes about what they have imagined. Tell them to start writing whenever they feel ready.

Play the music for at least five minutes. If people want more time to write, give them whatever time is needed.

When participants have completed their notes, ask them to share their visions, offering one element or aspect at a time. Ask for a volunteer to start, and then go around the circle until each person has shared as many times as she or he would like.

Then engage participants in discussing the following questions:

- How much harmony is there among our visions?

- What would it be like to live in a world like the one we have just described?

At the conclusion of this discussion, take a 10-minute break.

Exploring 35-40 minutes

Organize the group into three small groups (or two small groups if you have eight or fewer participants), and give each small group a marker and a few sheets of newsprint. Post the three newsprint sheets of the questions you have already prepared. Ask the groups to discuss and respond to each question as much as they can in 20 minutes, devoting about seven minutes to each question. Ask them to seek consensus responses, but recognize that they may not achieve consensus in such a limited time. Ask them to list their responses on a sheet of newsprint.

Ask the small groups to begin. Tell them when seven and 14 minutes have elapsed. After 20 minutes, gather the whole group together. Invite a member of each small group to share her or his group's responses to the first question. List all of the small group's responses on the sheet of newsprint under the first question. (If a response is offered by more than one group, list it only once.)

Follow the same procedure with the responses to the other two questions. When you have listed all of the small groups' responses, explain that you are going to discover the whole group's orientation to these three questions. Give each person six stick-on stars, and ask people to put a star next to what they believe are the two most pressing needs on the needs list, the two most powerful obstacles on the obstacles list, and the two most powerful methods on the methods list.

Distribute the stars, and invite people to affix them. When they have done so, count up the stars and announce the results. Invite discussion about the results of the "voting."

Integrating 20-25 minutes

Select one of the options listed below for this activity.

Option 1

Ask participants to move into the same small groups they were in for the previous activity. Ask each group to choose some aspect of how a more peaceful and just world might actually be—and how it would feel to live in such a world—and to present a skit of three to four minutes depicting that aspect.

Give the small groups about eight minutes to prepare their skits; then have the groups present them. After all of the skits have been presented, invite reactions as time allows.

Option 2

Organize participants into small groups of three or four members. Ask each group to create a collage that portrays what a more peaceful and just world could be like 25 years from today. Make the collage materials available, and ask the groups to begin. Toward the end of the available time, have each group show its collage to the others and talk a little about its meaning for them.

Option 3

Engage participants in discussing what a profoundly more peaceful and just world would be like, how it would feel to live in such a world, and how the existence of such a world would change their daily lives.

Closing 3-5 minutes

Gather the group in a circle. Give participants a brief preview of the next session. Then place the chalice in the center of the circle and light it. Ask people to join hands around the circle. Say something like:

"Light is the ally of vision. Let me ask you now to look into the light of our candle... Look into the light before you, and ask yourself simply, how can I make a difference for peace and justice?"

Allow a minute of silence. Then extinguish the candle, and have participants break their circle of joined hands. Invite people to the social time.

Reflection and Planning

Consider the questions below, and discuss them with your co-leader(s):

1. What have I learned from the experience of leading this session?

2. What preparation do I need to do for the next session?

Session 6 ♦ How Do We Make a More Just and Peaceful World?

Goals for Participants

- to explore a commitment they can make to work for a more peaceful and just world
- to have an opportunity to make a commitment to act in a specific way to promote peace and justice in the world
- to feel a sense of closure to this program.

Overview

In this final session, participants first imagine ways they can contribute to the cause of peace and justice in the world and then consider contributions to which they may want to commit themselves. They explore some of the specifics of these activities with others in the group who are drawn to similar commitments. Finally, they are invited to make a commitment to some kind of peace and justice work during the next year.

As this is the final session of the program, you may want to arrange for more elaborate refreshments during the social time. Or, you may want to celebrate with a picnic, restaurant meal, or pot luck at a leader's or participant's home.

Materials

- Newsprint, markers, tape, and easel
- Writing paper
- Pens and pencils
- Copies of Handout 11 ("Norman Cousins Quotation")
- Newsprint poster of Handout 2 ("Program Goals") from Session 1
- Chalice, candle, and matches

Preparation

- Set up the usual circle, easel, and chalice.
- Photocopy Handout 11.
- Make appropriate arrangements for the social time.

Session Plan

Gathering 6-12 minutes

Greet participants individually as they arrive. When the group has gathered, ask people to join you in the circle. Engage them in a brief checking-in.

Focusing 5 minutes

Note that you'd like to read again the passage from Norman Cousins that you read during the first session. Then read aloud the passage below:

> The starting point for a better world is the belief that it is possible. Civilization begins in the imagination. The wild dream is the first step to reality. It is the direction finder by which people locate higher goals and discern their highest selves.
> —Norman Cousins

Invite responses, but keep the sharing to a few minutes. At the end of the sharing, distribute copies of the passage. Then give participants a brief overview of this session.

Reflecting   40-50 minutes

Distribute writing paper and a pen or pencil to each participant. Tell people that you are going to engage them in a guided imagery experience. Ask them to find a comfortable position, sitting up or lying on their backs, and to close their eyes. Then lead the guided imagery by saying something like:

"Now I would like you to let yourself relax... Take some deep, long, slow breaths. As you breathe out, feel the tension leaving your body... As you breathe in, feel relaxation flowing into your body. Breathe in this way for a few moments." (Pause for 15 seconds.)

"Now, on the count of three, I want you to tense every muscle in your body, hold them tense for a few seconds, and then let go. Okay, one, two, three! Hold it... Release. Okay, let's try that one more time. One, two, three. Hold it... Release.

"Now become aware of your feet, and feel the relaxation in them... Now feel that relaxation moving up from your feet into your legs, moving all the way to the top of your legs... And now feel that relaxation moving into your torso, into your stomach... Into your chest... and now up your back... Become aware of your fingers and hands, and feel them becoming relaxed... Now feel that relaxation moving into your wrists and on up into your arms... And now feel that relaxation into your shoulders... Into your neck... Into your jaw... Feel your face relax... Feel the energy of relaxation filling your head." (Pause for 15 seconds.)

"Now that you are calm and relaxed, I'd like you to imagine that you are about to go to a special place that you know about, a place that helps you to feel centered and wise. It can be a real place that you know or a place of your imagination... Now I would like you to go to that special place." (Pause for 15 seconds.)

"Now I would like you to be aware of this special place. Look around you, and see what there is to see... And now feel whatever the special qualities or energies of this place are." (Pause for 10 seconds.)

"You have come here to make a decision. You are going to choose a commitment you will make to work for a more peaceful and just world in a particular way. Let the possible actions you can take, the projects you can work on, the ways that you can help—let whatever kind of activity that calls to you come into your awareness now." (Pause for 20 seconds.)

"And now let one particular commitment, one particular kind of activity, rise up above all the others as the one you choose to do." (Pause for 15 seconds.)

"Now that you have chosen a way of acting for peace and justice, I would like you to imagine yourself acting in that way, working on that project, that commitment. See yourself working in that way in the next couple of weeks." (Pause for 15 seconds.)

"And see how you are enacting that commitment over the next couple of months." (Pause for 15 seconds.)

"Now you have progressed a whole year from the last session of this program at [your congregation]. It is now [the date one year from this day]. Let yourself look back at all that you have done over the past year to work for peace and justice in the way you chose." (Pause for 20 seconds.)

"Now I would like you to come gradually back in time... Back a little further... And now a little further... And now you have come back to this day. When you are ready, I would like you to return to this room and open your eyes. But please remain silent when you do."

When everyone has "returned," ask participants to write a letter to themselves from the perspective they experienced in the guided imagery when they were one year into the future. Ask them to describe what commitment they made to work for peace and justice and how they fulfilled this commitment.

When everyone has completed a letter, gather participants in a circle. Invite people to share summaries of their letters to themselves with the group.

When all have shared who wish to do so, invite people to share their reactions to this experience.

When this discussion ends, take a 10-minute break.

Exploring   35-40 minutes

Gather the group in a circle. Invite those who expressed an interest in similar topics, issues, concerns, or kinds of action to join together in small groups. Use your judgment to help people organize when interests do not match exactly. Be sure that each interest group has at least two people. Also, if anyone asks, tell people that they can join a group that is working with a different action or issue from the one they chose in their imagery if they wish.

Tell participants that you would like them to discuss how they can transform their imagined activity into commitment and action in the real world. Invite them to use this time to plan what they will do to work for peace and justice beginning tomorrow. Ask them to consider the following:

- Making a commitment to work on a specific project or action in collaboration with other members of this group, with others outside this group, or by themselves

- Creating an action plan for their peace and justice activity, with goals and a time frame.

Ask participants to begin their work. Let people know when they have about 10 minutes remaining for this activity. When time requires, gather participants in a circle.

Integrating 10-15 minutes

Invite each person or project group to share with the whole group what they have committed themselves to undertake. Invite others in the group to share ideas and feelings in reaction to the commitments.

Post the newsprint copy of Handout 2 and invite participants to discuss the goals in light of their experiences in this program.

Closing 8-12 minutes

Place the chalice in the center of the circle and light it. Have the group stand in a close circle around the chalice, with each person's arms around those standing next to her or him.

Share with the group some of your thoughts and feelings about what you have shared together in these sessions. You may want to thank participants for their involvement. Then invite them to share whatever they would like to tell others in this moment.

Close by singing "Shalom" or another appropriate song.

Extinguish the candle, and invite people to join in the social time.

Reflection and Evaluation

Consider the questions below, and discuss them with your co-leader(s):

1. What gifts have I received from the members of this group?

2. What gifts have I given the members of this group?

3. What have I learned from the experience of leading this program?

Please photocopy the two-page evaluation form at the end of this program, fill it out, and send it to the UUA Curriculum Office.

Optional Passages

We (Unitarian Universalists) have a gospel that relates to the process, the unitary oneness, the universal connection of all creation. This theology we need to articulate and to live out, so that we give a contemporary focus to our faith. At a time which Matthew Arnold summed up as "Wandering between two worlds, one dead, the other powerless to be born," we would leave the dead past to bury its own and take as our concern the birthing of the new world.

—Peter S. Raible

To live, Letting God do it.

Spread self-consciousness into concern for others.

Leave oneself an open door, a free unconscious channel,
for the deep rushing flood of life to pour through.
To tell and tell forever humanity's great secret—that each one
is all the rest, and each one can do the world's work.
A calmness born of the immeasurable power that moves us.
A rich Peace, seeing that life is good.
A joy, deepening daily as we understand.
And love—the love that all things live in—
To feel it and give it.
To give it. Give it. Give it everywhere.

Go in peace.

—Charlotte Perkins Gilman

The Music of Peace

(Peace) is the highest and most strenuous act of the soul, but an entirely harmonious action, in which all our powers and affections are blended in a beautiful proportion, and sustain and perfect one another. It is more than silence after storms. It is as the concord of all melodious sounds.... It is a conscious harmony with God and the creation.... An alliance of love with all beings, a sympathy with all that is pure and happy, a surrender of every separate will and interest, a participation of the spirit and life of the universe, and entire accord of the purpose with its Infinite Original. This is peace, and the true happiness of man [sic].

—William Ellery Channing

I am a part of all created things!
The power that rules the stars is manifest
In me and in my being is expressed
Unfathomable mystery that clings
To all the things that I behold. The heart
Of this strange universe beats with my own;
The sea flows in my veins; I am a part
Of hills and sky, yet separate, alone.
The light serene that has come from age to age
Sustained us on our earthly pilgrimage
Shines in my breast. Why should I be dismayed?
I will go forth where others too have trod
Undaunted, resolute and unafraid
And walk the earth star-crowned like a god.

—Muriel Hilton

See yourself in others.
Then whom can you hurt?
What harm can you do?

—Gautama Buddha

In your dedication to your own life's work, whatever it may be, live as though you had forever, for no amount of careful and devoted doing is too great in carrying out that work to which you have set your hands. Cultivate in your work and your life the art of patience, and come to terms with your inevitable human limitations, while striving also to extend the boundaries of your understanding, your knowledge and your compassion.... Know that although in the eternal scheme of things you are small, you are also unique and irreplaceable, as are all your fellow humans everywhere in the world. Know that your commitment is above all to life itself.... It is up to you now to do all that you can and that means a commitment, at this perilous moment in our human history, to ensure that life itself will go on.

—Margaret Laurence

Our future is prefigured in our imagination, and is dependent on our bringing post-modern ethics and politics concretely to bear as therapy for the wounds that bring so much pain to those with whom we share the planet. Taking suffering seriously is the best indication that we care about the future in a way that matters.... Unless we link our bodies and resources to the various struggles against specific crimes of modernity, we are not ethically and politically fit to cross the great divide linking present to future.

— Richard Falk in *The American Theosophist*, Spring 1987

Handout 1

Program Outline

Session 1: Orientation and Beginnings

Session 2: What Is the State of Peace and Justice in the World?

Session 3: Do We Choose Peace and Justice?

Session 4: How Do We Live a Just and Peaceful Life with Others?

Session 5: What Are Our Visions of a Just and Peaceful World?

Session 6: How Do We Make a More Just and Peaceful World?

Program Goals

- We will enlarge and sharpen our awareness of peace and justice issues.

- We will explore the threats to the survival of humankind and other life on this planet and consider our feelings about these threats.

- We will explore the connections between peace and justice in our decision-making.

- We will explore the ways that we deal with interpersonal conflict.

- We will explore the challenges of working to increase the quantity and quality of peace and justice in the world.

- We will choose to (re)commit ourselves to working for peace and justice in the world and will feel more empowered to do so.

Unitarian Universalist Principles

We believe in the following principles, and we join together to support them.

- We believe that each and every person is important.

- We believe that all people deserve to be treated with fairness and kindness.

- We believe that our churches and fellowships should be places where people accept each other and where we can learn and grow together.

- We believe that each person must be free to search for what is right and true in life.

- We believe that each person must be guided by her or his conscience, and that people should have a say in decisions that affect them.

- We believe in working for a peaceful, fair, and free world.

- We believe in caring for and taking care of our planet Earth.

Handout 4

Guidelines for Your Peace and Justice Story

Your peace and justice story is the story of your relationship to the issues of peace and justice throughout your life as well as your sense of where you are heading now in relation to those issues.

Your peace and justice story is likely to include some of the elements listed below. Please don't feel obliged to speak to all of these elements, but use the ones that are helpful to you.

- Recall your earliest memory of a peace and justice activity that you took part in or watched. What are your memories and feelings about this?

- As you were growing up, were you taught about what an ideal world would be like? If so, who taught you? Did you have your own vision of an ideal world? When, and what was it?

- Consider the heroines and heroes you had as a child, teenager, and adult who embodied your values and beliefs about peace and justice.

- Consider the activities that you took part in as a youth and young adult that related to peace and justice.

- How have the types of peace and justice activities that you take part in changed over the years? Why?

- What is your peace and justice activity level now? What would you like your level of activity to be?

- What image helps you to make sense of your efforts for peace and justice?

- The peace and justice issues that you care about most are…

Handout 5

Role-Play 1: Diane/David

You are Diane or David. You have worked in this factory for more than 30 years. You are now the production supervisor, responsible for production of the desired quantity and quality of men's shirts. It is one of your duties to assess the work of the employees.

Today you have called Jan to your office. Jan used to be a good worker. However, recently, by your estimate, he or she has not met the standards of production that you expect and has not demonstrated his or her loyalty to the company. You feel that you have really tried to address Jan's concerns about working conditions and that he or she has not appreciated your efforts.

Handout 6

Role-Play 2: Jan

You are Jan. You are an immigrant in this country who arrived only three years ago. You have worked in this factory for nearly a year.

You have recently raised the issue of the timing of coffee breaks with your co-workers. Now the rule is that everyone breaks at 10 a.m. You think that since the system of production is so individualized anyway, why shouldn't people be allowed to take the break at the time they choose? This idea was the subject of one discussion with the supervisor, but nothing came of this discussion.

Today you have been summoned to the supervisor's office unexpectedly. You are surprised by the unfriendly tone of her or his summons, because you know that you are one of the most productive workers on the floor.

Handout 7

Role-Play 3: Les/Leslie

You are the chairperson of your congregation's Social Justice Committee. This is a long-standing committee, but it shows signs of becoming active for the first time in many years under your leadership.

You believe that it is the committee's responsibility to focus the congregation's attention on some specific issues and concerns, and to mobilize the congregation into acting together to address these issues.

You know that not everyone on the committee agrees with you.

Handout 8

Role-Play 4: Robert/Roberta

You are a somewhat reluctant new member of your congregation's Social Justice Committee. You aren't sure that you really belong on the committee, but you have agreed to take part for a while because you are concerned that the new chairperson will cause the committee to act in a way that will generate profound conflict within the congregation.

You believe that the committee's role is to inform and educate the members of the congregation about social justice issues and concerns and, through education, to encourage people to get involved with these issues. However, you do not believe that the committee ought to try to get the congregation as a whole to support a particular cause.

Conflict Management Styles

Avoid: Ignore the conflict, pretend it does not exist, run away from it.

Accommodate: Meet the other person's needs before your own; give in because the relationship is more important than your needs.

Encourage: Try to understand the other person's viewpoint and help or uphold him or her at the expense of your own needs.

Compromise: Bargain, negotiate; both parties give up something of value.

Persuade: Try to talk the other person into changing her or his position or needs.

Compete: Try to win, to compel the other to accede to your will; meet your own needs, not the other person's.

Problem-Solve (Win/Win): Work together to find a solution that has the best results for both parties; requires genuine collaboration.

Guidelines for Win/Win Conflict Resolution

Win/win conflict resolution means that the people in conflict work together to resolve the conflict. This approach is also called collaborative problem-solving.

The win/win aspect of this approach means that both parties in the conflict experience a significant element of success or winning in the outcome.

All parties to the conflict must take the following steps for this approach to work:

1. Let emotions cool down before you start to work on the conflict. All parties must be ready and willing to work on the problem in a reasonable way.

2. Define the problem together. State the conflict clearly and openly. Acknowledge the real differences that exist.

3. Share feelings and needs related to the conflict, and listen carefully to the feelings and needs shared by the other party. Before a conflict can be resolved to the satisfaction of both parties, each party must know fully the feelings and needs of the other and must believe that the other person knows about her or his feelings and needs.

4. Jointly gather information needed for resolution of the conflict. Doing this together gives validity to the information and gives both parties an opportunity to work together successfully.

5. Brainstorm and list as many options as possible that might resolve the conflict in a win/win manner. This is not always easy. The key is to state and record as many ideas or options as possible through brainstorming. Be as creative as you can. Include options that may seem unrealistic or even silly at first, because they may lead somewhere.

6. Review all of the options raised, and select one by mutual consent. This assures shared commitment to the mutually developed and selected decision.

Two hints for using win/win approaches:

- Give the process enough time to work! Don't give up if it gets hard or takes considerable time. Remind yourself how valuable it will be to resolve the conflict successfully.

- Use humor whenever possible. Laughter frees people from fear, embarrassment, and anger, and creates a mood of hopefulness. It helps people to relax, let go of tension, and think more creatively and clearly.

The starting point for a better world is the belief that it is possible. Civilization begins in the imagination. The wild dream is the first step to reality. It is the direction finder by which people locate higher goals and discern their highest selves.

—Norman Cousins

Evaluation of *In Our Hands: Adults*

We need you! Help us serve you by sending us your comments, suggestions, and critiques of this program. Please photocopy this form, using additional sheets if needed, and send to: Curriculum Development Office, Unitarian Universalist Association, 25 Beacon Street, Boston, MA 02108-2800.

General Information

1. With what age group did you use this curriculum?

2. Approximately how many participants?

3. How many leaders?

4. Is there anything else you would like to tell us about your religious education setting? (very small or very large congregation, etc.)

General Comments

Please include comments on what worked, what didn't, and how you modified the program to fit your needs.

Comments on Sessions

Session 1: Orientations and Beginnings

Session 2: What Is the State of Peace and Justice in the World?

Session 3: Do We Choose Peace and Justice?

Session 4: How Do We Live a Just and Peaceful Life with Others?

Session 5: What Are Our Visions of a Just and Peaceful World?

Session 6: How Do We Make a More Just and Peaceful World?

Sample Sessions from Other Volumes in the Series

Provided here are sample sessions from the four other volumes of the *In Our Hands* series. They are included to give you an idea of the intergenerational nature of *In Our Hands*.

These sessions follow the streamlined format common to all volumes in the series: the simply stated Goals for Participants, the quick Overview, the handy list of Materials and Preparation steps, and the complete Session Plan—laid out in clearly timed subsections.

- From *In Our Hands: Grades 1-3*, "The Peace Quilt" involves the young children in a quilt-making project for the whole congregation. Based on the Boise Peace Quilt Project, the activities in this session are designed to encourage cooperation and the joy of gift-giving—while promoting the ideas of peace and justice.

- From *In Our Hands: Grades 4-6*, "Earth Awareness" invites the children to sample the amazing variety that exists in the natural world. The Exploring activities focus on each of the five senses individually. By deepening their appreciation of nature, the children feel more committed to their environment.

- From *In Our Hands: Junior High*, "Beginning a Peace and Justice Project" emphasizes making a commitment to peace and justice. The teenagers in this program are asked to consider how they could make a difference by cooperating with their peers on a group project—such as organizing a food collection, collecting toys or clothes for others, or setting up a peace and justice library for the congregation.

- From *In Our Hands: Senior High*, "What Peace and Justice Issues Face Our Generation?" helps maturing teenagers identify some problems they will have to address as they approach adulthood. Participants read two poems reflective of the world situation and brainstorm about peace and justice issues.

Grades 1-3

Session 15 ♦ The Peace Quilt

Goals for Participants

- to learn about a group of Unitarian Universalists and their friends who are helping to build friendship and peace today through the making of peace quilts
- to create a peace quilt and share it with the rest of the congregation.

Overview

The central activity in this session engages the children in creating a peace quilt that they can present to the congregation for hanging in your building. As an introduction to this activity, the children will learn about the quilting project begun by two Unitarian Universalists in Boise, Idaho.

If you are aware of similar or related projects by other Unitarian Universalists, you may wish to share stories about them with your participants.

Please note: Additional work is needed to complete the peace quilt begun in this session. Please see Preparation for a description of the adult help you will need to obtain.

Materials

- A copy of Handout 3, "Peace Signs" for each participant
- A few sheets of drawing paper for each participant
- Postcards of the Boise peace quilts (see order form at the back of this book), and a slide projector and screen
- A white or light-colored 12 x 12" block of cloth for each participant, and a few extra cloths
- Regular crayons
- Fabric crayons for drawing designs on the cloth
- A copy of the book *Long Neck and Thunder Foot* by Helen Piers (optional)
- Chalice, candle, and matches

Preparation

- At least a week before this session, recruit the following adult helpers.

    - one adult helper for every four or five children to help during the session itself

    - if desired, a helper to iron the crayon designs onto the cloth

    - a helper or helpers to stitch the children's blocks into a quilt with cloth strips between them or sewn onto a cloth backdrop, and to prepare the quilt for hanging

- If you are not familiar with fabric crayons, try them prior to this session so that you can teach the children how to use them effectively.

- Discuss with the appropriate persons in your congregation the time at which the group can present the quilt to the congregation and where the quilt can be hung. Perhaps it can be presented at the beginning or end of a worship service. Arrange to hang the quilt in a prominent location. Make these arrangements before this session so that you can tell the children about them.

- Set up your library table and at least one other activity for arrival time.

- Read through the information about the Boise peace quilters that follows and be prepared to tell the participants about this project.

The Boise Peace Quilt Project

The quilting project was the inspiration of two women who live in Boise, Idaho: Diane Jones and Anne Hausrath. Both are members of the Unitarian Universalist Fellowship of Boise, Idaho. Anne and

Diane were concerned about what the future might hold for their children. Diane thought of a friendship quilt, and Anne expanded on the idea. Through the quilting process they sought to bring people together to create a gift as an expression of their desire for peace. They spread the word and found 35 others who wanted to contribute to the quilts.

The project began in the fall of 1981. In the spring of 1982 the first Boise Peace Quilt, intended for a sister city in the Soviet Union, was delivered to the Soviet Embassy in Washington, D.C. The quilt was accepted with great ceremony. By 1989, 19 other quilts had been created, each taking many months and hundreds of hours of work. By now hundreds of people—women and men and children—have contributed to the project. The quilts are dedicated to peace-seeking individuals and groups and are given as gestures of goodwill.

The theme of the first Boise Peace Quilt is "Of Idaho and Peace." It is now in a Peace Museum in Vilnius in the Soviet Union.

The theme of the second quilt is "Families." It was designed from children's drawings and was given to Norman Cousins.

The theme of the third quilt is "All Things Precious, Idaho's Land and Life." It was given to the people of Hiroshima, Japan, and it hangs in a health-care facility in that city.

The fourth quilt is called "We'll Stitch This World Together Yet." It was given to Pete Seeger.

The theme of the fifth quilt is "Peacemakers." Each square represents a person or group dedicated to making the world a more peaceful place. It was given to Helen Caldicott.

The theme of the sixth quilt is Senator Frank Church, the former senator from Idaho who was always concerned with issues of peace. It was given to Senator Church three months before he died.

The theme of the seventh quilt is "the Web of Life." Each quilter contributed a "crazy" patch of significant fabric to match the "crazy quilt" effect created in the two-mile fence surrounding the Greenham Common Air Force Base in England. Women wove fabric pictures and mementos in and out of the cyclone fence to protest the placement of U.S. missiles in their country. The quilt was presented to the women of Greenham Common.

The theme of the eighth quilt is the "Soviet and American Children's Quilt." Each square is based on a drawing by either a Soviet or a U.S. child. The quilt was given to the Soviet people and now hangs in the Leningrad Hospitality House.

The ninth quilt is the National Peace Quilt, composed of 50 squares, one from each state and based on children's drawings. Many U.S. senators have slept under the quilt. Their names are embroidered beneath the block representing their state.

The tenth quilt, "Celebrate the Peacemakers," includes the names of special peacemakers in each peace dove block.

The eleventh quilt, "Katherine Pavesic's Quilt," was designed by developmentally disabled children and was presented to Pavesic, an exceptional local teacher.

The twelfth quilt, "The Boise Peacemakers Quilt," commemorates Boise peacemakers.

The theme of the thirteenth quilt, "Nicaragua Libre," is the right of the Nicaraguan people to choose their own destiny. This quilt was presented to an elementary school in Nicaragua.

The fourteenth quilt is the "Joint Soviet-American Peace Quilt," cooperatively designed and stitched by Soviet and American women. Women carried this quilt to speak its peace to Soviet and U.S. arms negotiators in Geneva, Switzerland.

The fifteenth quilt, pictured on the cover, is for Charles Clements, a Quaker doctor from the United States who served the people of El Salvador. It was presented to Dr. Clements in 1986.

The sixteenth quilt, the "Sanctuary Quilt," tells the story of refugees of Central America. It honors the refugees' situation as well as the communities in the United States that serve as sanctuaries for them.

The seventeenth quilt was presented to Elise and Kenneth Boulding. Elise is a sociologist who specializes in imaging the future; Kenneth is an economist and poet. The squares of the quilt show images of the world we want to create.

The eighteenth quilt is the fifth anniversary quilt of the Boise Peace quilters. Each square celebrates an adventure of the quilters. This quilt is often used as a teaching tool.

The nineteenth quilt was presented to John Jeavons, the founder of Ecology Action, and author of a book to bring back bio-intensive gardening, *How to Grow More Vegetables*. This technique of low-technology, high-labor gardening has allowed people in developing countries to reclaim land and produce a high yield of crops with less water. Each square is dedicated to individual gardeners, ecologists, and naturalists.

The twentieth quilt was dedicated to Archbishop Raymond Hunthausen of Seattle. The squares and scenes are pictures and symbols of his life.

Session Plan

Arrival and Centering 10-15 minutes

Invite the children to peruse the library table and/or to take part in the activity(ies) that you have prepared.

When the group has gathered, ask the children to join you in your semicircle. Introduce your adult helper(s), and have the children introduce themselves. Then invite each child to tell the group about a peaceful experience that she or he has had in the past week.

Focusing 2-3 minutes

Say something like: "At our last meeting we learned how some people in our own Unitarian Universalist congregation are working to make our world fairer and more peaceful. Today we'll hear a story about how several Unitarian Universalist women and their friends and children are using their quilting skills to work for peace."

Reflecting 6-10 minutes

Tell the children the story of the Boise peace quilters and show the postcards of the various peace quilts. Invite questions and comments about the story and the quilts. Then ask the children questions like the following ones:

- How do you feel about these peace quilts when you look at them?
- What do you think of the idea of making peace quilts?
- Do you want to make a peace quilt together this morning?

Exploring 18-25 minutes

Introduce the group project by saying something like: "Today we will make our own version of a peace quilt. It won't be just like the ones the people in Boise make, because those quilts take many months to design and sew. But it will be a quilt, and it will give us a way to show how we feel about peace."

Explain the quilt-making process to the children by saying something like: "Each of you will get a sheet of paper and a block of cloth. First you will draw a peace design on paper, using regular crayons. This will give you a chance to practice making your design. When your peace design is ready, you will draw it on the block of cloth, using special crayons for drawing on cloth. Then all of your designs will be stitched together to make the quilt. This stitching won't take place today but will happen [whenever you have arranged for it to be done]."

Ask for questions, and respond to any. Be sure that the children understand the process. Then hand out the copies of Handout 3, "Peace Signs." Ask the children to look at these signs. Explain to them that they may create their own designs for the quilt or they may use any of these if they like.

Invite the children to move to the worktable(s). Pass out the supplies, and ask them to begin. You and your helper(s) can guide the children through the process as needed.

Integrating 8-14 minutes

When they have completed their drawings on the cloth blocks, gather the children in your circle. Invite each child to show his or her drawing to the group and to describe it briefly.

When all have done so, you may want to ask the children to suggest how the blocks could be arranged in the quilt. The group might create an arrangement of the blocks, for example, on a table.

Ask the children if they would like to present the finished quilt to your congregation. If they would, explain how it can be done and how the quilt can be displayed.

If you wish and time allows, read aloud or tell the story, *Long Neck and Thunder Foot*. Engage the children in discussing the meaning of this story.

Closing 3-5 minutes

Place the chalice and the candle in the center of the semicircle. Have a child light the candle, and ask, "How do you feel about the peace sign you made today?" Invite responses.

When all have responded who choose to do so, engage the children in singing "Under One Sky." Extinguish the candle. Say goodbye to each child individually.

Grades 4-6

Session 14 ♦ Earth Awareness

Goals for Participants

- to become more aware and appreciative of the variety of things that share our environment
- to consider what life is and what its requirements are
- to become more aware of the environment through the conscious use of their senses.

Overview

In this session the children interact with the world in ways that encourage a greater awareness of their natural environment. They use all their senses to explore the world around them. Through heightened awareness, the children can deepen their feelings of appreciation for the variety and beauty of their natural environment.

Materials

- A bag of peanuts
- Large brown paper grocery bag for each child
- A Feelie Box for each child or pair of children (see Preparation)
- Smelly Containers (see Preparation) and a small square of cloth for each participant
- Materials for What's This White Stuff? (see Preparation)
- A collection of natural objects (rocks, shells, pine cones, flowers, fossils, etc.)
- A newsprint-sized poster of the lyrics to "We've Got the Whole World in Our Hands" (in Music)
- Chalice, candle, and matches

Preparation

- Set up your usual circle.

- Gather a collection of natural objects and display them on a table.

- Make a Feelie Box for each child or pair of children: Cut the top off a half-gallon milk carton or similar box. Put into the box objects like: smooth acorn, heavy rock, feather, soft cotton ball, nail, piece of sandpaper, sticky Lifesaver, penny. Cover the top of the box with a sheet of paper, taped on, or with an old athletic sock. (Each Feelie Box must contain the same eight objects.)

- Make a Smelly Container for each child or pair of children: Gather a number of 35 mm film canisters or similar small plastic containers. Put a different one of the following or similar pungent materials in each one: toothpaste, body powder, orange peel, pine needles, sawdust, cinnamon, bug repellant cream, peanut butter, chalk, and so on.

- For What's This White Stuff? have eight to ten powdery white substances, each in its own clear glass container. Substances can include sugar, baking powder, salt, confectioner's sugar, baking soda, starch, flour, and so on. *Be sure that all can be tasted safely.*

Session Plan

Centering   4-7 minutes

Greet the children individually as they arrive, and invite them to examine the natural objects displayed on the table.

When the group has gathered, ask the children to join you in a circle. Then say something like: "We'll begin today with another kind of Centering. Let your body settle down now and find a place where it feels comfortable and supported.... Close your eyes, and remember to keep them closed throughout this activity. Now let your body feel peaceful and relaxed.... Take a few slow, deep breaths, and let the tension drain out of your body." (*Pause for ten seconds.*)

"Now become aware of your eyes." (*Pause for five seconds.*)

"Move your eyes slowly up and down, but be sure to keep them closed.... Now move your eyes slowly from side to side.... Now move your eyes in a circle.... Now imagine that you are seeing through the center of your body." (*Pause for ten seconds.*)

"Feel yourself relax a little more.... Now become aware of your ears.... Let your ears pick up all of the sounds that you can hear outside this room.... Now pick up all the sounds you hear that are inside the room.... Now listen to the sounds inside your ears." (*Pause for five seconds.*)

"Pay attention to the way that you breathe. Breathe out slowly through your mouth, and breathe in slowly through your nose. Let's try it. Breathe out slowly. Get all the air out.... Now breathe in through your nose. Get all the air in.... Now breathe out. Feel the tension leaving your body.... Now breathe in. Feel energy coming into your body.... Now try it again. Breathe out.... Breathe in.... Breathe out.... Now breathe in, and feel the energy flowing into your body. Let the energy flow through your body, making you awake and alive and alert." (*Pause for ten seconds.*)

"Now that you are full of energy, I'd like you to come back to this room, and open your eyes when you are ready. Then move your feet and hands a little. And gently sit up, and then carefully stand up and stretch as tall as you can and feel all the energy in your body. Be sure to do each step slowly and carefully."

Focusing 5-7 minutes

When all of the children are standing, gather them in your circle and ask them to sit. Explain that you will begin to explore peace and justice in a different way today: peace and justice with the earth. Give them a brief overview of this session.

Ask the children what senses they explored in the centering activity. Note that today they will have an opportunity to explore their environment through their senses.

Ask the children to define the meaning of *environment*. Then ask them to give examples of environments in which they live, for example, this room, the town or city, home, school, your region, North America, earth, this solar system. Help them move from the particular to the global and beyond.

Reflecting 10 minutes

Say something like: "We all live in and are a part of many different environments. Right now we are in our classroom environment. Everything in this environment, or any environment, can be divided into three groups: living, non-living, and once living but no longer alive."

Then ask these questions one at a time, and invite responses:

- What is there in this environment that is living?"

- What is there here that once was living but is not living any longer?

- What is there that is non-living?

- What does it mean to be alive?

Introductions

Then say something like: "There are four things that all living things need to stay alive. I'll introduce them, and you tell me what they are."

Read aloud or say in your own words the introductions below, giving the children time to identify each one.

(In a gentle voice) "I taste so good when you're all sweaty from riding your bike. I fill your swimming pools, but I'm much more important than that. I rain on all the trees, flowers, and grasses. And I'm a large part of what makes up every living thing."

(In an energetic tone) "Imagine wearing every coat and blanket in your house and still freezing! That's what would happen without me. I heat the earth, and I give you light, too. My energy gives energy to every living thing on your little planet."

(With a blowing tone) "I am everywhere you look. Touch your face—you just squeezed me. Breathe in and out—that's me. The breath of life!"

(With a squeaky voice) "Wait a minute, wait a minute! Don't forget me. Everybody walks all over me, but I hold up everything. And I feed all of the plants, and they feed all of the animals. Nobody could live without me!"

(Answers: water—sun—air—soil)

Exploring 25-30 minutes

Say something like: "Now we are going to explore our environment with our senses, so tune up your ears, open your eyes, wiggle your noses, and stretch your fingers." Then do as many of these activities as time allows.

Explore a Peanut

Give a peanut to each child. Ask the children to look carefully at their peanuts: to find a hump, a valley, a bump, a scar, a dent, a ridge, the smoothest part, the roughest part, and so on. Ask them to consider how long the peanut is, how many colors it has, and what shape it is.

Give each child an opportunity to introduce his or her peanut to the group. Then put all of the peanuts together on a table, and ask the children to find their own peanuts. When all have done so, invite them to eat the nuts.

Listen to the Sounds

Go to an area inside or outside, weather permitting, that is *not* dominated by one sound. Ask the children to listen carefully to all of the sounds that they hear. Ask them to be aware in particular of which sounds are made by living things and which are made by non-living things.

Hand out the grocery bags. Ask each child to put a bag over her or his head, close her or his eyes, and listen.

After a minute or two, have the children open their eyes and remove the bags. Ask what sounds they heard and what feelings they had in reaction to the various sounds.

Feelie Boxes

Pass out a Feelie Box to each child or pair of children. Describe one of the objects in the boxes *without naming it*. Ask the children to find that object *without looking into their boxes* and to take the object from the box. When all of the children have removed the object, invite them to give its name. (If two children are sharing a box, have them take turns.)

Follow this procedure with several objects, and then engage the children in discussing how they find the described object without looking.

Then follow the same procedure with the remaining objects.

Smelly Containers

Gather the children in a circle. Have the Smelly Containers in front of you. Open one, and cover it with the square of cloth. Ask each child to smell it as the container is passed around the circle. Be sure that the children keep the container covered with the cloth, so they can't see the contents. When all of the children have smelled the container, invite them to identify what place they associate with this smell. Then ask them to identify the substance. Do the same with the other containers.

What's This White Stuff?

Gather the children in your circle. Have the white substances available. Pass one of them around, and ask the children to see if they can identify what it is only by looking at it. Have everyone hold their guesses until each child has had an opportunity to examine the substance. When all have looked, have the participants share their guesses, and then tell them the answer. Discuss with the children how they identified or tried to identify the substance.

Have the children close their eyes. Tell them that you will pass around another white substance and that you want them to see if they can identify it only by taste. Follow the same general procedure. Demonstrate the use of the two senses by passing around the other substances.

Integrating　　　　　　　　　　5-8 minutes

Lead a discussion using these questions:

- How did you become more aware of your environment by paying such close attention to your senses?

- What happens when we pay attention to one sense and ignore the others?

- Can we pay careful attention to all of our senses at the same time?

Closing　　　　　　　　　　3-5 minutes

Give the children a preview of the next session. Then place the chalice in the center of your circle. Have a child light it. Allow a moment of silence, and then say:

"Today we'll close by singing a song that talks about how we relate to our environment, although often we don't think of it quite like this."

Point out the lyrics of "We've Got the Whole World in Our Hands," and lead them the children singing some or all of the song. Have a child extinguish the candle. Say good-bye to the children.

Junior High

Session 10 ♦ Beginning a Peace and Justice Project

Goals for Participants

- to review the Unitarian Universalist story and vision they explored in previous sessions
- to make a commitment to enacting a peace and justice project, to select their project, and to begin work on it.

Overview

In this session participants first review some of what they have learned about the Unitarian Universalist story and vision for peace and justice. Then the session invites them to make a commitment to work on their own peace and justice projects in the context of this program.

It is essential to the value of this experience that the young people perceive this invitation as a genuine one, so that their decision to do a project is a genuine choice on their part. Structure this decision so the majority of the group rules. The most likely scenarios include the following:

- Everyone in the group wants to do a project. With this outcome, you have no problems!

- The majority wants to do projects, but one or a few do not. With this outcome, ask the one or few to go along with the choice of the majority.

- The majority does not want to do projects. With this outcome, omit the projects as an activity and revise this unit accordingly.

Please note that projects can be done individually or in pairs and trios. Prior to this session, consider the skills and characteristics of your participants, and decide if you want to let them choose how to group themselves for the projects, or if you wish to provide guidance in that process.

Materials

- Copies of Handout 7, "Unitarian Universalist Forebears," and Handout 8, "Project Ideas"
- Pens and pencils
- Scratch paper, stationery, envelopes, and stamps
- A writing surface, such as a book, magazine, or clipboard, for each participant
- Markers, paints, and other art media
- Construction paper, tagboard, and newsprint
- Glue, tape, and scissors
- Chalice, candle, and matches

Preparation

- Set up your usual circle.

- Set up the work tables and chairs.

- Review the "Project Ideas" and, if you wish, add ideas to the list before you make copies.

- Consider the guidance you want to give the young people as they choose projects. For the project activity, have one adult as a resource for every five or six participants. If you need to recruit assistants for this project, be sure they know that this involvement is for three sessions. Prior to the session, brief your assistant(s) about the session plan. Give them copies of the handouts, and discuss with them the purpose of the projects, the kinds of projects that are appropriate, and their role as the assistants.

Session Plan

Gathering   8-10 minutes

Greet the young people as they arrive. When the group has gathered, ask people to join you in the circle.

If you have assistants, introduce them to the group and explain their role. Ask people to describe something that happened to them in the past week that surprised them.

When all have shared who wish, engage the young people in playing an active game.

Focusing   10-12 minutes

Gather the participants in your circle. Briefly review what the group has done so far. Note that this session marks the start of the final unit in this program, and give the participants an overview of this session.

Have the young people organize themselves into pairs and trios. Hand out the pencils, writing surfaces, and Handout 7. Ask participants to work in pairs or trios to fill in the blanks with the correct names. Note that this activity reviews some of the stories they have heard about Unitarians and Universalists who contributed to making peace and building justice. Ask them to begin.

When the pairs and trios have finished, gather the group in a circle. Go over these answers:

1. Clara Barton
2. William Howard Taft
3. Benjamin Rush
4. Susan B. Anthony
5. Adin Ballou
6. Horace Mann
7. Mary Livermore
8. John Haynes Holmes
9. Dorothea Dix
10. Theodore Parker
11. Julia Ward Howe

Welcome questions and comments about any of these persons.

Reflecting   4-6 minutes

Ask the participants to consider the following question: "Of the 11 Unitarians and Universalists we have just identified, which person is the most interesting to you, and why?"

Pause for a minute, then invite people to share their responses.

Exploring   8-12 minutes

Explain that you are going to invite the group to work on peace and justice projects, beginning today and concluding in your final session. Tell the young people that it is their decision whether or not to do projects. Explain that the majority of the group will rule in this decision.

Note that you would like them to decide about the projects in a few minutes, but first you would like the group to brainstorm a list of possible projects so they know what their decision is about. Review the rules for brainstorming.

Post a sheet of newsprint, and ask participants to suggest possible project ideas. Write all of the suggested ideas on the newsprint.

When the group has run out of suggestions, distribute Handout 8. Invite people to look over these sheets, and check any ideas that interest them that have not already been suggested. Give participants time to read the lists, then have them share the ideas they have checked. Add new ideas to the brainstorming list.

Now invite the group to make a decision about doing projects. Explain that choosing to do a project involves making an effort to work for peace and justice and that it is important that people be clear that they want to make this commitment. Facilitate discussion as needed, and help the group arrive at a decision. Then respond to the group's decision according to the guidelines in the Overview.

Integrating   15-25 minutes

Ask participants to indicate with a show of hands who wants to work alone and who wants to work in a pair or trio. Then have those who wish to work with others form pairs and trios.

Invite the participants to choose a project. Ask individuals, pairs, and trios to raise their hands when they have made a choice, so they can tell you (or your assistant(s)) what they have chosen. The leaders need to hear all the choices before participants begin to work, so you can be sure that each project selection is appropriate for this context and can be completed in the time available. Then, as time allows, help the young people begin to work on their projects. Make the various materials available. Circulate among the young people, and provide aid and encouragement.

Closing 4-7 minutes

When time requires, have participants clean up. Then have them gather in a circle. Tell people that they will have time during the next two sessions to work on and finish their projects.

Give the group a brief preview of the next session. Then place the chalice in the center of the circle and have a participant light it. Say, "May this flame remind us of the power that we have to contribute to making peace and building justice among the people we know, and in the larger world."

Allow a few moments of silence. If desired, engage the group in singing a song. Then have a participant extinguish the chalice. Say goodbye.

Senior High

Session 9 ♦ What Peace and Justice Issues Face Our Generation?

Goals for Participants

- to identify what they perceive to be the most important peace and justice issues facing their generation
- to share their understanding of and feelings about these issues
- to choose to explore one or more of these issues in greater depth
- to reflect on a vision of a peaceful and just world.

Overview

This session helps participants identify what they think are the most important peace and justice issues their generation will face. The activities involve them in sharing their beliefs and feelings about the meanings and implications of these issues.

This session offers the group a springboard from which to create additional sessions. If participants wish to explore one or more issue(s) in greater depth, work with them to plan and enact additional sessions.

This topic may provoke powerful emotional responses from participants. Reflect on this possibility prior to the session and be prepared to be helpful and supportive in whatever ways are appropriate.

Materials

- Newsprint, easel, markers, and tape
- Copies of the poems by Josephides Panayiota (Handout 11) and Judy Chicago (Handout 12)
- Chalice, candle, and matches

Preparation

- Set up your regular circle and easel.
- Make copies of the two poems for each participant.

Session Plan

Gathering   12-15 minutes

Greet participants individually as they arrive. Invite them to peruse the Resource Table.

When the group has gathered, engage the participants in a brief checking-in. Give people a short overview of this session, and distribute Handout 11.

Note that the Panayiota poem was written by a 17-year-old from Cyprus. Have a volunteer read the poem aloud. Invite people to respond to the poem by asking questions like the following:

- Do you agree with the sentiment expressed in this poem? If so, why? If not, why not?
- What feelings do you have in reaction to this poem?

Keep this discussion brief, unless people express a strong desire to discuss the poem at length.

Interacting   15-20 minutes

Organize the group into sub-groups of three. Give each sub-group a marker and sheet of newsprint. Then say something like: "Many people see the times in which we live as a time of world crisis. We hear about different parts of the crisis almost every day in the news. There are so many issues and problems that sometimes it all feels overwhelming. But on the most basic level, it seems that all of these issues and problems can be seen as issues of peace and justice."

Invite reactions. Then say: "What I'd like you to do in your groups is discuss what you see as the most important, most critical issues of peace and justice that face the world today. Talk about this question for awhile — what the issues are, what the problems are — and then list the three or four most critical ones on your sheet of newsprint."

Be sure that participants understand the task. Then ask them to begin. Give them time to create their lists. When they have done so, have the groups post their lists on the wall.

Invite participants to examine all of the groups' lists. Then ask the group to create a new list that ranks the various issues according to how many times each one appears on the small group lists; for example, if "avoiding nuclear war" is on four lists and "preserving the Earth" is on three lists and no other issues are on more than two lists, the former is #1 and the latter is #2, and so on.

Investigating 20-25 minutes

Note the issue that is ranked first by the group. Tell participants that you are going to ask them to take part in a values line. Lay out the imaginary line as you did in Session 1. Then put the #1 issue as listed by the participants into the form of a question, as in this example: "What do you see as the likelihood of avoiding a nuclear war during your lifetime?"

Identify one end of the values line as "total confidence that nuclear war will be avoided" and the other end as "certainty that there will be a nuclear war." Be sure that participants understand what each point represents. Then repeat the question, asking people to take a place on the line that represents what they believe.

When participants have taken a position on the line, invite them to look at the distribution of the group. Encourage comments and reactions to this distribution, and encourage this interaction to become a discussion of the issue itself, as time allows. As part of this discussion, raise the following questions:

- What can people do about this issue or problem?

- What can we do about this issue or problem?

Follow this procedure with at least two more issues, as listed by the group. If time allows, explore others as well.

Engage the group in discussing the following question: "Are there ways in which these issues or problems are connected with each other?" If they cannot do so themselves, help participants gain a sense of the relationships among various peace and justice issues.

Integrating 10 minutes

Engage participants in considering whether they would like to explore any of these issues in greater depth. If they would, begin to plan how the group will proceed.

You may need to complete this planning at the next session. With any additional sessions, involve participants in the planning and leadership as much as possible for your group.

Closing 5 minutes

End the discussion and give people a preview of the next session. Place the chalice in the center of the circle, and have a participant light it. Ask people to look at the flame for awhile and then close their eyes and allow themselves to become receptive. When all have had their eyes closed for awhile, tell them you are going to share a poem with them that you'd like them to reflect upon. Then read the Judy Chicago poem aloud.

Allow some moments of silence. Ask people to open their eyes. Close with a ritual that is appropriate for your group.

Pass out copies of the Judy Chicago poem as you say goodbye to the participants.

Social Action Organizations and Resources for All Ages

These social action organizations are key resources for any peace and justice effort. Browse through this list for ideas on how to help. For an extensive listing of social action organizations, consult *Resolutions and Resources: A Social Responsibility Handbook,* available through the UUA Bookstore.

Adopt-A-Stream Foundation
P.O. Box 5558
Everett, WA 98201
Guidelines and activities for students to adopt a stream in their community.

Afro-Am Educational Materials
819 South Wabash Avenue
Chicago, IL 60605
An excellent source of books, games, toys, filmstrips, music, etc. that features African Americans and other people of color. Send for catalog.

Alternatives
P.O. Box 429
5263 Bouldercrest Road
Ellenwood, GA 30049
(404) 961-0102
Nonprofit educational organization that provides resources for responsible celebrations and lifestyles, raising consciousness about the connection between affluence in this country and poverty here and abroad; publishes a catalog, holiday packets, bulletin inserts for churches, and a quarterly magazine.

The American Forum
Education in a Global Age
45 John Street, Suite 1200
New York, NY 10038
(212) 732-8606
National resource center on global education. Provides teacher training programs, curriculum materials and guides, consultants, speakers, conferences, and the newsletter *Access.*

American Friends Service Committee
1501 Cherry Street
Philadelphia, PA 19102
(215) 241-7000
Operates a criminal justice program which works for social services for families of prisoners, prisoners' education, restitution for victims, alternatives to incarceration, and the abolition of the death penalty; also works on conflict resolution.

Amnesty International
304 West 58th Street
New York, NY 10019
(212) 582-4440
Independent, worldwide movement working impartially for the release of all prisoners of conscience, fair and prompt trials for all political prisoners, and an end to torture and executions.

Ark
250 Lafayette Circle, Suite 301
Lafayette, CA 94549
(415) 283-7920
Institute founded on the hopeful vision of ordinary citizens' playing a role in preserving their planet. Programs and books available.

The Asia Society
Education and Communications
725 Park Avenue
New York, NY 10021

Beyond War
222 High Street
Palo Alto, CA 94301
(415) 328-7756
National nonprofit educational organization interested in educating about survival; works locally, nationally, and internationally to discuss, develop, and demonstrate a new way of thinking; publishes a monthly newsletter, *On Beyond War,* and educational materials.

Birthday Friends for Peace
P.O. Box 15514
Pensacola, FL 32514-5514
Matches Soviet and American pen pals by their birthdays. Send 3" x 5" card with name, birthday, and mailing information. Small donation accepted.

William C. Brown Co.
Publishers/ROA Media
2460 Kerper Boulevard
Dubuque, IA 52001
(800) 922-7696
Publishes *Cooperative Learning, Cooperative Lives: A Sourcebook for Building a Peaceful World*. Over 100 classroom activities and projects promoting an understanding of cooperation.

Children Around the World
P.O. Box 40657
Bellevue, WA 98004
(206) 643-0172
Resource center to help schoolchildren around the world connect with one another.

Children of the Green Earth
P.O. Box 95219
Seattle, WA 98145-2219
(206) 525-4002
Educational organization sponsoring tree-planting partnerships with school and community organizations around the world.

Children's Creative Response to Conflict
P.O. Box 271
Nyack, NY 10960-0271
Activities, publications, and workshops to promote skills of cooperation, communication, conflict resolution, and mediation.

Citizen's Clearinghouse for Hazardous Wastes
Box 926
Arlington, VA 22216
(703) 276-7070
Provides direct support to community groups and small municipalities dealing with hazardous waste problems.

Concerned Educators Allied for a Safe Environment
17 Gerry Street
Cambridge, MA 02138
(617) 864-0999
Newsletter, workshops, slide show.

Cooperative Learning Center
202 Pattee Hall
University of Minnesota
Minneapolis, MN 55455
(612) 624-7031
David W. Johnson and Roger T. Johnson, Co-directors.
Conducts research on cooperative learning and provides training to teachers, administrators throughout the world. Newsletter: *Cooperative Link*.

Council on Interracial Books for Children
1841 Broadway
New York, NY 10023
(212) 757-5339
Develops public awareness of racist, sexist, and handicapist stereotypes in children's books and learning materials.

Crossing Borders (video, 32 min.)
Film Project for Women's History & Future
P.O. Box 578447
Chicago, IL 60657
Film chronicling the 70-year history of the world's oldest women's peace group. Rent or purchase.

Cultural Diversity Festival
One of five full-color posters available from The Education Program of the John F. Kennedy Center for the Performing Arts. Printed on high-quality, heavy stock and suitable for framing. Costs $8.95 each; plus $2.50 postage and handling. The Education Program of JFK Center for the Performing Arts, Washington, DC 20566.

Directory of Alternative Travel Resources
One World Family Travel Network
Dianne G. Brause
P.O. Box 3417
Berkeley, CA 94703
(415) 841-TRIP
List of alternative and socially conscious travel options, opportunities, and organizations.

Drops of Water, Grains of Sand
(video, 25 min.)
Peace Links
747 8th Street SE
Washington, DC 20003
(202) 544-0805
Citizen diplomacy—US/Soviet women's exchange. $15.

Earthseals
P.O. Box 8000
Berkeley, CA 94707
Stick-on stamps, four-color view of the planet from space. 7/$1 or "whatever feels appropriate."

Educators for Social Responsibility
23 Garden Street
Cambridge, MA 02138
(617) 492-1764
Publishes books and distributes videos on world issues. Membership includes quarterly newsletter *Forum*.

Everyone's Kids
71 Elliott Street
Brattleboro, VT 05301
A bibliography of multi-racial books for children of all ages. Send for catalog.

Facts on File, Inc.
460 Park Avenue South
New York, NY 10016
Global Guide to International Education resource book of information on programs, organizations, and publications in global education.

F.O.W.L.
P.O. Box 477
Petaluma, CA 94953
Information from a group of young people working to save endangered species. The how-to's of starting a wildlife club in your neighborhood or school.

Friends of Earth
530 Seventh Street SE
Washington, DC 20003
(202) 543-4312
Promotes preservation, restoration, and rational use of the earth.

The Giraffe Project
45 West Street, Suite 402
New York, NY 10036
(800) 344-TALL
An organization devoted to spreading the word about those willing to "stick their necks out"—through the media and their quarterly publication. $25 membership includes a year's subscription to the *Giraffe Gazette* and copies of monthly radio stories.

Global Cooperation for a Better World
P.O. Box 325
Boston, MA 02146
Offers *Cooperation in the Classroom*, a project for teachers.

Global Education Associates
475 Riverside Drive, Suite 570
New York, NY 10115
(212) 870-3290
International network working for global harmony. Educational programs, AV materials, and quarterly publications.

Global Links
WETA-TV
Educational Activities
P.O. Box 2626
Washington, DC 20013
(800) 445-1964
Six-part videotape series on social and economic development in the Third World. Teachers' guides and supplemental material available.

Greenhouse Crisis: The American Response
Union of Concerned Scientists
26 Church Street
Cambridge, MA 02238
Ten-minute video outlines the consequences of the greenhouse effect and offers concrete actions students can take to reduce pollution and slow the effects.

Green Teacher
c/o Lisa Glick, Lifelab
809 Bay Avenue
Capitola, CA 95010
Resource published in Britain. Focuses on environmental education.

Green Times
2-1645 E. Cliff Drive #40
Santa Cruz, CA 95062
(408) 476-6389
A quarterly resource guide to whole earth studies. $15/yr.

Greenpeace
1611 Connecticut Avenue NW
Washington, DC 20009
(202) 462-1177
Promotes ocean ecology, disarmament, and an end to toxic pollution.

Habitat for Humanity
Habitat & Church Streets
Americus, GA 31709
(912) 924-6935
Nonprofit organization dedicated to engaging the affluent in partnership with the poor to help low-income families build and own their own homes; gives technical assistance and training to its local affiliates.

Healing Community
139 Walworth Avenue
White Plains, NY 10606
(914) 761-4986
Helps congregations of all faiths to become accessible in attitude, architecture, and communication to persons with disabilities and handicaps; conducts workshops and consultations; provides resource publications and a quarterly newsletter.

The Holyearth Foundation
P.O. Box 10697
Bainbridge Island, WA 98110
(206) 842-7986
Creates international person-to-person opportunities and newsletter *The Earthstewards Network*.

Institute for Defense & Disarmament Studies
Ballinger Publishing Co.
Cambridge, MA 02138
Publishes *Peace Resource Book*. Guide to issues, groups, and literature on peace and disarmament. $14.95.

KidsArt News
P.O. Box 274
Mt. Shasta, CA 96067
Newsletter of creative art activities, kids' contributions, and fold art from many cultures. $8/qrtly.

Little Friend for Peace
4405 29th Street
Mt. Rainer, MD 20712
Offers *Creating a Peace Experience* (a resource guide for setting up a peace day camp) and *Peacemaking for Little Friends* (activities around 12 themes plus bibliography).

MEND
P.O. Box 2309C
La Jolla, CA 92038
Mothers Embracing Nuclear Disarmament.

National AIDS Network (NAN)
1012 14th Street NW, #601
Washington, DC 20005
(202) 347-0390
National resource center for AIDS education and service delivery with 300 community-based constituent service providers; offers technical assistance, education support, and help with service programs to persons with AIDS; publishes a biweekly, *Network News*, and a monthly, *NAN Multicultural News*.

National Alliance Against Racist and Political Oppression
126 West 199th Street, #101
New York, NY 10026
(212) 866-8600
Broad-based coalition of church, political, labor, civic, student, and community organizations committed to organizing millions of people to repel the growing repression of leaders and activists in movements for freedom, peace, and justice.

National Audubon Society
950 Third Avenue
New York, NY 10022
(212) 832-3200
Works to preserve the quality of life on earth through the protection of wildlife, land, water, and other natural resources—and to solve global problems.

New Society Education Foundation
P.O. Box 582
Santa Cruz, CA 95061-0582
A source of excellent global education resources—including books, programs, and calendars. Send for catalog.

Northcote House
Eastover Road
Plymouth PL6 7PZ, UK
Publisher of *International Peace Directory*. More than 1000 entries which include the name, address and telephone number of organizations that exist to promote peace.

Northern Sun Merchandising
2916 East Lake Street
Minneapolis, MN 55406
A fine source of peace and social justice posters, T-shirts, buttons, etc. Send for catalog.

One Sky
Saskatchewan Cross-Cultural Centre
134 Avenue F South
Saskatoon, Saskatchewan S7M 1S8
Canada
(306) 652-1571
Provides the latest information on women, indigenous people, and other Third World development issues of importance to Canadians; publishes reports, books, and pamphlets and maintains a film rental and periodical library.

Opposing Viewpoints
Greenhaven Press, Inc.
577 Shoreview Park Road
St. Paul, MN 55126
(800) 231-5163
Book series in a pro/con format presenting national and international issues.

Our Only Earth Youth Summits
19428 Aurora Avenue North, Suite 425
Seattle, WA 98133
(206) 546-5760 or 652-9502
Information on creating Youth Summits that address global concerns.

Oxfam America
115 Broadway
Boston, MA 02116
(617) 482-1211
Nonprofit international organization that funds self-help development projects and disaster relief in Third World countries; also prepares and distributes educational material for Americans on issues of development and hunger.

The Peace Garden Project
P.O. Box 5282
Elmwood Station
Berkeley, CA 94705
A grassroots movement to build a national peace park in Washington, DC.

Peace Letter
Children of the Earth Foundation
231 East La Jolla
Tempe, AZ 85282
A new quarterly newsletter supporting Peace in Education.

Peace Links
747 Eighth Street SE, Department L
Washington, DC 20003
(202) 544-0805
National organization of women against nuclear war. Outreach programs for schools; packets for planning a Peace Day celebration and for starting high school Peace Links groups.

Peace Packet
Institute of Noetic Sciences
475 Gate Five Road, Suite 300
Sausalito, CA 94965
(415) 331-5650
Contains readings and suggestions for inner and outer work in finding one's own role in the quest for global peace.

PeaceTrees
Holyearth Foundation
Len Laviolette
7624 Potrero
El Cerrito, CA 94530
Reforestation project raises funds to promote programs for Soviet and American teenagers to work in partnership with an emerging nation.

Posters for Peace
A set of four full-color 18" x 24" posters with themes of peace is available through the children's book council. Created by artists from four cultures. Each order ($23.50) contains an annotated "Books for Peace" listing, which includes books for young readers that promote peaceful ways to resolve conflicts. Order from: Children's Book Council, P.O. Box 706/67, New York, NY 10276.

Skipping Stones
A Multi-Ethnic Children's Forum
80574 Hazelton Road
Cottage Grove, OR 97424
(503) 942-9434
A quarterly magazine which accepts original writings and artwork from children of all ages, in every language. $15/yr.

Social Science Education Consortium, Inc. (SSEC)
855 Broadway
Boulder, CO 80302
(303) 492-8154
Publishes curriculum guides for global education in elementary and junior and senior high schools.

Teachers College Press
1234 Amsterdam Avenue
New York, NY 10027
Publishers of books on Peace Education, including *Educating for Global Responsibility: Teacher Designed Curricula for Peace Education* and *Comprehensive Peace Education: Educating for Global Responsibility* (both by Betty Reardon of Columbia University).

United Nations Association of the USA
485 Fifth Avenue
New York, NY 10017-6104
Model UN and youth programs.

US—USSR Youth Exchange Program
3103 Washington Street
San Francisco, CA 94115
(415) 346-4234
Exchange programs include wilderness adventures on both continents.

Valentine Vision
50 West Cedar Street
Boston, MA 02114
(617) 523-5329
An organization promoting activities on Valentine's Day which "imagine a world where no child goes hungry." Provides informational packets for planning classroom and school participation.

Volunteers for Peace, Inc.
43 Tiffany Road
Belmont, VT 05730
(802) 259-2759
Promotes global cooperation through voluntary service in peace and environmental overseas work camps.

Wish List for Peace
Frances Weinstien
Hammond Public Library
564 State Street
Hammond, IN 46320
An eight-page annotated bibliography of books which offer peaceful ways to resolve conflicts. Send a self-addressed 9" x 12" envelope with 45¢ postage.

WorldWatch Institute
1776 Massachusetts Avenue NW
Washington, DC 20036
Independent, nonprofit research organization analyzing issues from a global perspective and identifying global trends.

Youth Ambassadors of America
P.O. Box 5273
Bellingham, WA 98227
Exchange programs, conferences, and summits for young people. Newsletter: *The Bridge*, $12/yr.

Zephyr Press
P.O. Box 13448, Department F8
Tucson, AZ 85732-3448
A clearinghouse for a wide variety of creative learning materials—including books, games, and other resources. Send for catalog.